You'll never know how

You'll never know how

For Sam and Ruth *cum amore*

By the Same Author
A THOUSAND FRIENDS
I LAUGHED, I LOVED, I CRIED

DOROTHY FULDHEIM

A Thousand Friends

Doubleday & Company, Inc.
Garden City, New York
1974

Copyright © 1974 by Dorothy Fuldheim
All Rights Reserved
Printed in the United States of America
First Edition

Library of Congress Cataloging in Publication Data

Fuldheim, Dorothy.
  A thousand friends.

  CONTENTS: What is TV really like?—Aunt Molly.—Talk shows and
hosts. [etc.]
  1. Fuldheim, Dorothy. 2. Journalists—Correspondence, reminiscences,
etc. I. Title.
PN4874.F77T48   070.1′9′0924
ISBN 0-385-01701-4
Library of Congress Catalog Card Number 73–10805

The stories are of people I have known though the names have been changed, for some of them are still living. I have alternated them with some of my television experiences and reactions to this unique and overpowering medium. I've been broadcasting on TV for twenty-seven years doing news commentaries and interviews. The world has passed through my office and I found it a good world with thousands of friendly people.

DOROTHY FULDHEIM

Cleveland, Ohio

Contents

What Is TV Really Like?

There are no holidays for what are known as "talent" performers. I am at the studio on Christmas and all the other holidays as usual. Doing three shows a day takes time, my day at the studio starts at nine-thirty and doesn't end until six-thirty. There may be some newscasters who come in just to read their scripts, which have been written by someone else, but not in my case. I write two editorials a day and that takes time—not only for reflection but to gather material. I read nine newspapers a day plus magazines and books at night. I'm a rapid reader and unless the material is scientific data unfamiliar to me, I can scan an article very quickly and decide whether it contains information that I can use. People say I have a photographic mind. Nothing could be farther from the truth. I do not have a photographic mind, I do not remember words and phrases but I have almost a prehensile mind which grasps and holds onto facts and stores them away like a squirrel gathering nuts until I need them.

Holidays are gloomy because only a skeleton crew is on duty to take care of the live shows. This particular Christmas the day was overcast, it was bitterly cold, the machine which dispenses canned soup and sandwiches was empty. It was a doleful day and I was idly wondering what editorial would be fitting on Christmas Day when the porter came in with a large box. "Here's a present for you," he said.

"There's no delivery today," I said. "Where did this come from?"

He shrugged his shoulders. "I don't know. Some guy drove up in a Lincoln and said I was to deliver this to you."

I opened the box and after getting rid of all the tissue paper, I lifted out an exquisite chinchilla wrap—no small gift. The card read, "To brighten your day." No name. Just the initial—*P*. I was bewildered. I knew of no one that would be sending me such a munificent gift nor did I know anyone with that initial. The mystery continued. On New Year's Day a magnificent array of flowers arrived with a similar card, "To brighten your day." Each holiday brought a gift and always with the same card. Once it was a pearl necklace; another time, a black velvet dress with white mink. Then a basket filled with strawberries and pomegranates; still another time a jeweled evening bag. I was frustrated. Who was the giver—a man or a woman? I never knew because after two years of lavish gifts I received a corsage of violets and this time the card read, "This is to say good-by." It remains a mystery, I never have found out who the giver was.

Through the years I have been the recipient of some quaint and lovely gifts. One was a lace collar, the kind made by hand and bought in Belgium. The note accompanying it moved me to tears. "My husband," the note read, "bought this for me on our honeymoon. I'm alone now. He is gone, and I have no family, but it would delight me if you will wear this." I did and wrote her that I would cherish it.

I have a friend—breezy, highly intelligent, with a Ph.D. —who was converted to Catholicism at the early age of seventeen. She entered a convent; after twenty years she left, though remaining a devout Catholic. Robes billowing around her, she often sailed into the TV station accompanied by a student. Without waiting to be announced, she would storm my door. I learned from experience that her lovely smile, her enchanting ways resulted in my yielding to her request and she always had a request.

"All right," I would say, "what is it now?"

"There are a few books in your library that my class could use," or, "Listen, there is a family that I know of who need two winter coats—one for the mother and one for the youngster in my class. You wouldn't want them to be cold all winter, would you?"

"Of course, I wouldn't!" How could I disagree with her? She got the coats and was not above reminding me a few weeks later that they had no boots and wasn't it a brutal winter. She was the greatest con artist in the world but never for herself. I used to groan when I saw her coming into my office.

The house occupied by her and the other nuns was in a mixed neighborhood. It was an old house that had been repaired and converted into a convent for the use of the nuns. From the outside it looked like any other house in the run-down neighborhood. The nuns served as a teaching order for the school near by.

A lady of some promiscuity occupied the house next to the convent and as a result the doorbell was constantly being rung by some male who mistook the convent for the house with the promiscuous woman. The nuns were distressed. They were awakened at all hours and there is no doubt that the males who sought entrance were as aghast at having the bell answered by a nun as the nuns were bewildered by the variety of males who, apparently, mistook their house for the one next door. My husband, learning of their distress, looked into the matter.

"Don't you have a light over your door so the number can be identified?" No, they didn't have a light. It was too expensive having the necessary wiring installed. So my thoughtful husband instructed an electrician to put a light over the door and make it visible so the nuns would not be bothered by any of the men searching for the woman next door.

The electrician, eager to help the nuns and, apparently, not familiar with the origin of the phrase "the red light district," placed a huge red light over the door. Baffled by the increasing number of males who rang their bell all night long, the nuns complained to the police. The red light was removed. I accused my husband of a hilarious enjoyment of the nuns' plight. He used to retell the story with great delight.

For reasons that had nothing to do with her faith, my friend left the order. Then she had to find a job, make a home, and learn how to dress. It was amusing watching her adjust to a free, undisciplined life. It took a number of years but now she has friends in all walks of life.

One day we lunched together and she said, "Do you remember the turquoise bracelet and ring you gave me when I left the convent?"

"Of course I remember."

"Well," she said, "I sold them because I needed money, and I always felt guilty about it. Today I have something for you." And from her purse she brought out a large topaz set in handsome gold. "It's for you," she said. "Put it on."

"It's beautiful," I told her, "but where did you get the money to buy it?"

"Don't worry," she reassured me. "It cost very little; it's hot stuff."

Procuring guests is no longer a problem. It becomes a way of life for celebrities and people in public life to expect to be approached and interviewed. When I wanted to interview Willy Brandt, my director phoned his office in Berlin and told him when I would be there. A time was agreed upon, which we then confirmed by letter. A month later I was in Berlin, and according to our instructions, went to the municipal building. In the room where we were told the interview would be held we set up our lights and at exactly ten o'clock, as had been arranged over the transatlantic phone, Herr Brandt appeared and we taped the interview.

In the dramatic mayoralty campaign in Cleveland in the fall of 1973 the Democratic candidate, Jim Carney, announced his withdrawal from the race on a special show. Having completed that show, I rushed off to Severance Hall where the Cleveland Orchestra was opening its season. Mayor Ralph Perk, against whom Mr. Carney was running, was in attendance, and I wanted to get him on my show that night to express his feelings about the dramatic withdrawal of Mr. Carney. The question was how to steal the mayor. I knew his driver, so out to the parking lot I went. I got into the mayor's car and sent his driver to the box where he was sitting with a note saying, "I'm sitting in your car, it's important that you join me at once." He came, we drove to the studio, and I was able to do a follow-up program with Mayor Perk.

Leopold Stokowski, that vital man, who at ninety-three
was still active, delighted me, and after my interview with
him, I invited him to my home to have dinner with my
family. He expressed a desire for Hungarian goulash. To
obtain the goulash I phoned one of the Hungarian restau-
rants and arranged to have some delivered to my home.
He was a real gourmet. I've never known anyone else who
ate food and drank wine with a greater zest. He was one
of those fortunate beings who enjoyed every moment of
his existence and eating was a charming ritual for him. He
spent the major part of the evening talking long distance to
his wife, Gloria Vanderbilt, who informed him that evening that she was divorcing him.

Chill Wills and I became great friends at our very first
meeting when I interviewed him. It is strange the strong
attraction one feels for certain people—it has nothing to do
with sex. It is above and beyond that. One feels a great
tenderness, a sense of understanding and belonging to certain people, and it may be man or woman. When he returned to California, he called me and introduced his wife
to me via long distance so that she could at least talk to me.

One year while I was on vacation my daughter, who is
said to resemble me, substituted for me. When I returned,
I found a letter from a gentleman who wanted to know
where I had my face lifted because I had been looking so
much younger. He would like the doctor who performed
the surgery to do the same for his wife. It was with great
glee that I wrote him that the doctor who had performed
my face-lifting no longer was in practice. I saw no reason
why I should tell him the truth. When I went back on the
air, he must have been convinced that the doctor did a
bad job.

I never use make-up. I'm allergic to most of it because of the lanolin component. For a while I tried fake eyelashes. They were marvelous and I felt like an irresistible beauty as I fluttered them. I became absolutely coquettish, I was so enchanted with my looks; but, alas, I'm allergic to the glue, so all my beauty faded and I was obliged to become my unadorned self. Imagine a nation being so rich that we can afford to spend seventy million dollars a year on false eyelashes. As for having my face lifted, I've had a number of specialists in the art of lifting sagging muscles offer to perform such an operation on my face. I'm told it's simple but expensive. I always ask, "What about my hands? Can you restore the round fullness of youth? And what about muscles in less obvious places, such as around the waist? But most of all can restoring muscles restore the appetites of youth?" It is, I presume, the passionate desire to retain the appearance of youth, without which one is supposed to be without sex appeal. If that is so, I have transcended such limitations. The passionate quest for young flesh by older men is unfathomable to me unless one was limiting his association only to the bedroom —but the days are long. I've been told authoritatively that the Duchess of Windsor has had so many face lifts that to make the muscles of her face tighter might interfere with her swallowing. One of the saddest pictures any photographer ever caught was the Duchess, frail and mournful, walking up the ramp of the plane leaving England, where she left the body of the duke who loved her enough to give up a kingdom.

When I interviewed Lillian Gish, who might have slipped right out of the nineteenth century with her charm and her ladylike manner, she protested because of the lights. Like Gypsy Rose Lee, she said, "Do you allow these harsh lights? Do you know these bright lights wash out blue eyes? The planes of everyone's face differ and, therefore, need special lighting." I thought how right Miss Gish was when I saw Barbra Streisand, that unbelievably talented performer. Though she is anything but beautiful, with certain lighting she looked absolutely angelic. Any number of times I've told our engineers that I'm not eighteen, but they go on exposing me to the same lighting that they use for children and young, beautiful women.

Then there is the problem of my clothes. If I wore white, the lightmen groaned. If I wore black, they lost their minds. Where in heaven's name did they expect me to find pastel shades? Now at last we have new cameras that take all colors. Nevertheless, certain materials and patterns photograph better—velvet, satin, and contrasting patterns are best. I once bought a suit with small checks; wearing it on TV made the checks crawl. It was a disaster.

Clothes also are getting more and more expensive. My limit for a dress was once $150, but that's no longer true—$250 is more like it. When I was a young girl of thirteen or fourteen, I used to watch the sunsets and dream of being able to have a dress of every color visible in the sky. The public library which I used to visit twice a week to draw books (it was three miles from where we lived and although carfare was only three cents, we were too poor to afford it and I always walked back and forth) had a marble stairway and I would walk down the steps imagining that I wore a green taffeta dress with a train that rustled as I walked. I've worn a green rustling dress and I've had the many colored ones and now if I had the emotional capacity to want something as badly as I did in my young days, I would want the lace dress Barbra Streisand wore which probably cost five thousand dollars. It's obvious that there is always something we cannot achieve.

I've faced many crises while broadcasting. One devastating experience was with a bee. There it was buzzing around my head. I have to struggle to control myself. I was afraid to move for fear the motion of my head would frighten the bee into piercing my face with its stinger. On another occasion a fly trumpeted its buzz around me as I was broadcasting. It was maddening. Providentially for me, one of our floormen is an expert fly catcher. I don't know how he does it, but with a swoop of his cupped hand he can catch the most evasive fly. On this occasion he not only caught the fly but kept it alive and presented it to me at the end of the broadcast. He named the fly Evelyn and thereafter whenever a fly was visible it was always referred to as Evelyn.

I've broadcasted when I've had a raging headache, when a close member of my family was dying, and never revealed my own inner anguish, but the time I was really thrown and couldn't go on was when in the midst of the famous *One O'Clock Club* show, which was the first of the live variety shows between Chicago and New York, I was interrupted with a bulletin that John Kennedy was assassinated. I was stunned. I read the bulletin and said, "I can't believe it!" So he was gone, the man who for a short while had added glamour to the presidency. No one knew then of the strange doom encircling the Kennedy family nor that from that day forth there would be anguish, disorder, and distrust for our nation.

John Kennedy, Martin Luther King, Robert Kennedy, the assassination attempt on Governor Wallace, the unbelievable horror of Watergate and Agnew and Nixon, and to top all of that the realization that the earth was becoming like Mother Hubbard's cupboard—empty for the first time. There was a scarcity of all products in the land—copper, wheat, meat, oil, and gas. Was this the drum sound of doom? Had Malthus' prediction come true, only more ominously than even he envisioned it?

It seemed absurd and silly to go on with a gay program when John Kennedy lay dead, destroyed by a bullet. (Where were the gun lovers then?) The show must go on is a tradition of the theater. During the Second World War, Beatrice Lillie, in private life Lady Peel, was about to entertain the troops when the commanding officer offered to call off the performance because he had just received word that her only son had been on a ship bombed and sunk by the Germans. True to tradition, Miss Lillie replied, "No, I'll go on; I'll cry tomorrow." So we went on with the show but not with much feeling or enthusiasm—our thoughts were with the dead President.

I've never had an unlisted telephone but some of the calls are weird. At two o'clock in the morning the phone rang and a hysterical voice said, "Miss Fuldheim, I'm so worried. I don't know what to do. I'm not married, and I'm pregnant." At that time of the morning I wasn't feeling very friendly and I snapped, "You may be pregnant, but not on my time."

Another night at about one o'clock some woman called, I thought, to discuss my editorial. I was so annoyed I stopped talking and put the receiver down next to the phone. Thoroughly angry and wide awake I began to read when my buzzer rang. There stood two policemen. I looked bewildered. "Oh," they said, "you're all right, Miss Fuldheim."

"Well, why shouldn't I be? What made you think I wasn't?"

"We had a call from some woman who thought you had fainted or died because in the midst of a conversation, you stopped talking."

At that moment the night watchman came panting up the steps. He had seen the police and thought they were burglars in disguise. What could I do but invite them in for coffee. Once they left and I got back into bed, the phone rang again and it was the same woman who sent the police. If I was all right, could she discuss my editorial? This at two o'clock in the morning. I work my head off to perfect an editorial and I get a call not to express admiration for my thoughts but to inquire where I bought the blouse I was wearing.

Listeners call about their problems, an increase in their light bill; an argument about the age of the governor; how can they prevent another bar in their neighborhood; how can they survive on their pensions; why do I support the right of abortion; the oil shortage is phony—just to enable the oil companies to make more money, would I come to their daughter's wedding even though I don't know them personally because I would show their daughter's in-laws that they could have a celebrity on their guest list and if I would come, they would pay for my time; was I for impeachment of the President? What's the good of a Social Security increase if landlords raise the rent? The calls are really a panorama of people's needs and problems.

The one I love best was from a woman who told me she talks to all her plants and because of that they grow and grow. Her poinsettia plant is six feet and she calls it Murphy. She talks to Murphy and kids with it. Well, Murphy is getting so tall it won't fit into her house, so she told Murphy that she would have to give it away.

"Murphy," she said, "I want to give you to someone who is kind and will love you. Would you be happy with Dorothy Fuldheim?" Murphy, she told me, swayed slightly, which meant yes, it would like to go to Dorothy Fuldheim. Who could resist Murphy even if it is a giant by now?

Television is powerful. On my program we helped settle a transit strike, which was crippling Christmas trade. We helped prevent a teamsters' strike. We presented the Duke of Windsor, Marian Anderson, Arnold Toynbee, Walter Lippmann, a man whose stature ennobled the nation long before talk shows became part of our life style. Critics said TV would kill books, the contrary happened. More books are sold today than ever before. We were the first station to allocate time for books every week and we are constantly interviewing authors and discussing their works. TV probably does more than any form of advertising to accelerate the sale of books. The first day my book *I Laughed, I Loved, I Cried* came out hundreds were sold.

It isn't all milk and honey because I take positive stands on controversial subjects. I have been threatened with bombs and death a number of times. After the Kent State episode, threats to kill me were serious enough to necessitate police protection. Just a short while ago, because of something I had said, the station received word that my home was to be bombed that night. The manager called me to tell me about the threat and that they had alerted the police. I was already in bed and decided bombing or not I was just too tired to worry about it. The police came. My granddaughter was crying, "I don't want to be bombed!" But I was just too tired to rise and wait for the crisis. So, the police watched and I slept. For the sake of accuracy, let me say that I was nervous for a number of days thereafter.

People call to express their disapproval of what I've said. It's astonishing how strong people's convictions are. When I do an editorial criticizing the right of everyone to have a gun, I'm deluged with phone calls and letters of disapproval. I've even had disapproving letters about Spiro Agnew. "How come," they would write, "if you are always for the underdog, you can't defend Agnew? What makes you so prejudiced?"

One day a woman came in and asked for me. She had a long carving knife to kill me because she said I was destroying her head of hair, and so was Arthur Godfrey. But since she couldn't get to him, and I was accessible, I was to be the victim. I didn't know what she meant, but it was a frightening experience. The police took her away, and I collapsed.

I've never learned to shrug my shoulders at nasty calls. Sometimes I lose my temper and I snap back. After every broadcast there are calls; usually I take them. Many callers will explain, "Oh, I never thought I'd get to talk to you—just your secretary." But I'm always available. How will I know what people think if I don't talk to them? These conversations are one of the reasons I am practically unerring in my ability to foretell who will be elected both in local as well as national elections; people relay their anxieties by their questions.

I'm frequently asked how I got on TV. There is a certain logic to the steps that brought me there. Because it was a new media I was able to formulate my own pattern. No one knew that TV was to become the most powerful influence in the world—it educates—it entertains—it persuades—and has become the formidable weapon of men in public life. I was on radio for a number of years and did a unique program. It lasted for an unbroken hour—no commercials. I did the story of historical personalities—Cleopatra, George Washington, Maximilian, Marie Antoinette, Alexander Dumas, Rasputin, Sarah Bernhardt—at least one hundred of these biographies, all historically accurate. History can be taught in this fashion, changing the isolated and remote figures into people that lived and loved and suffered indignation and frustration as all of us do. Bismarck no longer remains a dead figure when the fact is known that, riding to a meeting with the king to plot the Franco-Prussian War, he was munching on some sausages that his wife had packed for him herself, not trusting it to a servant; to discover that Marie Antoinette's decapitated head revealed that her hair was white not from worry but because she had no dye to maintain the color makes her real. George Washington refused pay as commander in chief, but his expense account was monumental. The last of the Hapsburgs slept on an army cot but a carriage was sent out every morning to purchase two particular rolls that he liked for his breakfast—a carriage, a footman, and a coachman to buy two warm rolls.

I did programs without notes and always ended the historic biographies with the death of the individual whose life story I was reporting. When I started the death scene, the announcers who had gone out for coffee knowing they had at least an hour would come back into the booth aware that I would be finishing. Some of the educators wanted me to put these biographies together in a book but I never got around to doing it.

I did an hour on the life of Lenin. Immediately I was accused of being a communist, as though doing the life story of Michelangelo made me an Italian. (Not that I would object to it. I am devoted to the Italians, I like their outgoing quality of friendliness.) The accusation made the front page of the *Plain Dealer*. How silly it all seems now! But what I said then was more prophetic than I knew.

"The Soviets," I said, "will never be satisfied until they demote the free enterprise system into a secondary role imposing communism on the world! They have started and, like some dreadful scourge, have swallowed Estonia, Latvia, Lithuania, East Germany, Poland, Hungary, Czechoslovakia, and wait like hungry beasts to consume the Arab nations who unwittingly opened their arms to them."

Later I did news analysis on a radio station and then an editorial every Saturday on ABC radio sponsored by the Brotherhood of Railroad Trainmen. It followed the New York operas. When a Wagnerian opera was performed, it was always touch and go whether they would get off on time. Milton Cross never knew how nervous I was waiting for his last words.

I was doing a great deal of lecturing in those days and was invited to join the Scripps-Howard radio and TV station. Since there was no formula to follow, I formulated my own—a news show with comments and interviews. Because we were the first TV station between New York and Chicago, we commanded a huge audience. Though the number of TV sets was limited, listeners were not. Neighbors came to the homes of those who had TV sets to watch the shows; bars were crowded with TV watchers. Many a man was heard to say, "I can't stand a woman giving the news." This was before the women's movement became official. So great was the attention given to TV that when I went off to Taiwan to cover the evacuation of the Tachen Islands crowds came to see me off.

When Mr. Perris, now the brilliant manager of the Scripps-Howard station in Cleveland, and I left for Cyprus and Egypt crowds saw us off with singing and flowers. The head of the station once explained why he approved of me. "I can call that woman at midnight and tell her to leave at nine the following morning for Asia and she never says, 'I can't until I have my hair set.'" What he didn't know was that I never have my hair set. When I get out of

my shower, I simply comb it and brush it. The first time I
had my hair set was when I returned from Taiwan—that's
about seventeen years ago. Sent off to the Orient with a
few hour's notice, I would protest that I needed some shots
only to be told, "Get them on the way." I did. I've had
doctors in Italy, Greece, Iran, and India; I prefer to have
them in the U.S.

On one trip I had to change planes in Honolulu. As I
disembarked, I was greeted by the governor with leis and
kisses. Slightly bewildered as to why I was receiving the
Red Carpet treatment, I discovered he thought I was Senator Margaret Chase Smith, who also was on the plane. The
governor had kisses left for her but the leis were around
my throat.

If television has been a demanding experience, it has also
been an extraordinary one; achievers, thinkers, writers,
have passed through my door. My position in TV has enabled me to share noble and great thoughts from an Arnold
Toynbee to a Billy Graham, from a Walter Reuther to a
worker in a Ford plant, from a president like Truman or
Nixon to the parking lot attendant.

Who could have a richer life? I have watched television
grow into maturity. I have seen commercials change from
fairy tales showing only beautiful women to real women.
I remember one particular commercial which revealed a
young, exquisite girl with her yellow hair turning to gold
under the glow of the sun, dressed in chiffon, sailing
through the woods with birds chirping, flowers growing
at her feet, music playing, and a male with his arm around
her who had a torso so magnificent it would have put the
ancient Greeks to shame—both floating through the woods
to the sound of music. And where were they going? To
buy a box of detergent! Now commercials are short

dramas in which people look like and act like people. And if a woman is shown waxing her floor, she looks like a woman and not a debutante. Admittedly, some of the commercials tax one's credulity, like the ad showing initialed men's pajamas—it's obvious that if a man doesn't know who he is by the time he is ready for bed, there is something the matter with him.

To be part of a newsroom, to listen to the sardonic conversations of the reporters who have learned to question everything and everyone, to observe their meticulous reporting, to be part of a news team made up of four men and myself, gives one an unusual perspective of life. It's a unique association, although being the only woman does isolate one a bit. It is also true that being a woman enables me to ask provocative questions that a man couldn't get away with. My aim in conducting an interview is not to ask embarrassing questions or to top my guest. Since every individual has a story my purpose is to cut through and allow the personality of the guest to emerge like a cameo, clear in outline and structure, to discover what he believes, what he knows, and what he has done to distinguish himself. In my twenty-seven years I have interviewed almost fifteen thousand persons. That is surely what may be described as a massive acquaintance.

Aunt Molly

My aunt Molly, who was the most extraordinary woman I have ever known, was in tears; her third husband had died. The whole family was with her and the children she'd taken under her wing when she'd married their three fathers. She was grief-stricken and distraught. She needed a black hat and no one in the family had one.

"But why, Aunt Molly? What difference does it make whether you wear a black hat or a dark brown one? What earthly difference can it possibly make?" I asked.

"Do you hear that, Bertha [her sister and my mother], what your daughter is saying? What difference will it make? I should go to the funeral of my third husband and wear a brown hat! If it were my first husband or even my second, but for the third! How would it look if I wore a brown hat, I ask you?" she demanded.

There was no use in arguing with Aunt Molly. A black hat she would have to have.

Kenneth, Molly's second husband's son said, "All right, Aunt Molly, you will have a black hat." So he proceeded to haul out the black shoe polish liquid and covered Aunt

Molly's brown straw with the black polish and then presented it to her.

"What about the white flowers?" asked Aunt Molly.

"Give it back," ordered Kenneth, and he proceeded to paint the flowers black.

"Now," I said, "you've ruined the hat. Where else can you wear it?"

"With Molly's luck, her fourth husband will die; and she can have a hat ready," my mother said.

At this Aunt Molly turned and rose from her chair and addressed all of us. "You should all listen to me and hear what your aunt Molly has to say. You, Kenneth, who are the eldest, and Robert and Douglas and you, my sister; and you, my brother Sam; and you, my niece turning to me—on this day I call on God to listen to me. I know what God wants. Maybe He doesn't speak to me like He did to Moses, but this is not the ancient times. But He spoke to me. 'Molly,' He said, 'you are not ever to get married again because whoever you marry will die.' I am telling all of you, my sons, my nieces, my sisters, and brothers— no more marriages for me."

We were silenced. It was true that this was Molly's third husband and each one of them had died before the end of the second year of their marriage. To hold God responsible for their deaths, that we could understand, but to say that God had doomed Molly and that for some inscrutable reason known only to the Deity any man she married was doomed to die left us all in consternation.

My mother said, "Another Moses. And when did you speak to God that you know all this?"

By this time Molly was wringing her handkerchief. "To you He would have to speak. But to me, He doesn't have to use words. Am I such a fool that I don't understand Him? Tell me, if you are so smart, who else do you know

who has buried three husbands? Mrs. Ginsburg's husband
lost a foot. They had to cut it off. Did he die? No, he
wears a false foot. Mrs. Epstein's husband had pneumonia.
Did he die? The doctors gave him up but what does Mr.
Epstein do? He gets better! But me, Molly, has buried
three husbands in six years. When my Al got sick, the doctor said, 'Don't worry, he'll be all right. But my Al isn't
Mr. Epstein. As soon as the doctor left what does my Al
do—he opens his eyes and says, 'Coffee, Molly,' and dies.
Whoever heard of a husband asking for coffee and then
dying? Who else do you know? Whoever heard of such
a thing that a man with two eyes that can see should fall
down an elevator shaft? Why in all the United States of
America does my Sol have to step into an elevator that
isn't there? You tell me why."

"But, Molly," remonstrated her brother, "other husbands die. You are not the only one who loses a husband!"

Molly turned on him. "Sure, sure I know other husbands
die, but if you are so smart, tell me one other woman who
you know who has lost three husbands."

We were silenced.

"You see, there is a curse on me. I'll wear this hat this
time, and I'll never wear it again because I'll never marry
again."

"You shouldn't talk so silly," said Sam. "You are not
God."

"So, I'm not God, but I won't get married and I'll take
care of the nine boys, and I'll be a father and mother to
them."

Her family protested, "Molly, nine boys—you'll go
crazy."

"So," said Molly, "what should I do with them? Throw
them out on the street? I'm a rich woman now. Bill left
me five thousand dollars; Al, three thousand dollars; and

Sol, eight thousand dollars. On sixteen thousand dollars the boys and I will live."

The oldest was thirteen and the youngest was five. In the early 1900s that was a lot of money, but the family warned her that she would have trouble with the boys.

"Me?" said Molly, "I've had trouble—three husbands—God has done enough to me. I've agreed no matter what—no more husbands. So, God should please let me alone." She always talked about God as though He were a relative.

Molly never did marry again, but that didn't keep her from attracting men. Molly had a wide, smiling mouth with beautiful white teeth. She explained that her white teeth were due to the fact that she ate an apple every night.

"Who told you that, Molly?" we asked.

"Never mind who told me. I know."

How could we argue with that unshakable bit of information. Her teeth were white, said Aunt Molly, so who was right, she asked the rest of us. Her auburn hair was piled high on her head and babylike tendrils of curls surrounded her neck and forehead. Her eyes were violet and her deep bosom was white and soft as a swan's breast. Her laugh was deep and rich. She was a true original. The nine boys, left her by her three husbands, adored her and stared wide-eyed at some of her ideas.

The nine children retained the religions of their three different fathers, and they all had to go to church. Since there was only an Episcopalian church in the neighborhood—that's where they all went—the Baptists and the Jews—nine of them to the Episcopal Sunday School.

When they moved, the nearest church was Seventh Day Adventists. This was too much for the boys. Aunt Molly listened to their objections.

"They are all dumb," said Michael, just thirteen years

old. "You should hear some of the silly things they tell us."

Molly's sister listened. "Molly," she said, "for you it is a sin to send Sol's boys to a Seventh-Day Adventist Church. He will turn over in his grave."

"So," said Molly, "how will he know? If you know so much about what Sol is doing in his grave, maybe you can tell me how I can get all nine of them in a synagogue—the Baptists and the Episcopalians. I'll have trouble with a rabbi. You should know he'll ask questions, and questions I don't want."

"All right, Molly," said her sister, "Sam and I will take Sol's three sons to the temple."

"So," said Molly, "that leaves the Episcopalians and the Baptists. I could send them to Catholic Sunday School, that's close by."

"Why do we have to go anywhere?" asked Michael. "You don't go to the temple, Molly, why should we?"

"Listen to him," said Molly. "Already at thirteen he knows everything."

"Well, why, Aunt Molly, why?"

"Why?" said Aunt Molly. "Do you want the neighbors to say I'm not fit to bring you up without a father? Please, Michael, do me a favor and go to church. All right, I don't go, but how can I go when I'm not sure why God took my three husbands away and your father, too, may he rest in peace."

Michael went, Molly had secretly bribed him, though the other children didn't know about it. Michael was always something special.

"He's a dope," said Reginald, the Baptist. "Why doesn't he just go to his church without asking so many questions,"

Molly told the boys that Michael would surely be a great lawyer someday because he read so many books. As a mat-

ter of fact, Michael did not become a lawyer. He was
wounded in the First World War and carried a cane and
walked with a limp for the rest of his life. He was Molly's
joy and when he graduated cum laude from Yale she could
hardly contain her pride. She sat in the front row, as did all
the boys, nodding the plumes on her hat with joy.

Molly had a novel way of handling the nine. Whatever
they earned would be pooled and the eldest was to go to
college first. When he received his diploma, he was to help
the next boy.

In school, the boys made up a gang of their own and as
a result were very powerful. They never had any trouble
because when fights broke out on the school ground, they
banded together. All through their mature years they retained a strong loyalty to each other. They adored Molly
and she returned their affection.

The time came when Molly ceased to mourn and she began fluttering her eyes and her sensuous and gorgeous
body. An Italian builder fell in love with her violet eyes,
her auburn-colored hair, and her really beautiful figure.
But Molly wouldn't marry him.

"Why?" he demanded. "I can take care of you. You will
never have to worry, and we can send the boys back to
their fathers' families. They are not your obligation."

Molly turned on him, "I should send the boys back! Al,
and Sol, and Bill would turn in their graves! Never!"

"All right," said Francisconia Valedarapona—that was
his monumental name—"keep them. Taking care of them
will be my wedding present."

"All right," said Molly, "a present is fine, but not a wedding present."

"Why not? What's wrong with a wedding present? Do
you want to keep them?" her suitor asked.

"Nothing should be wrong with a wedding present, but there should be no wedding."

"Why, Molly? I want you. Do you want to see my credentials? I'll take you to the bank, and they'll show you my credit is good."

Molly shook her head. "No. If I marry you, you will die."

"Are you crazy? What do you mean I'll die? What kind of talk is that?"

So, Molly told him about her three husbands who died. She knew that God meant she should not get married again.

"First of all," Francisconia told her, "you don't know what God intends, and, anyhow, I'll take a chance. I'll pray to my God."

"You think the Catholic God won't let you die? You don't know what my Jewish God will do. I know. I won't marry you."

"Well," said Francisconia, baffled by her strange logic, "so let's live together without a wedding ceremony."

Molly thought that was a great idea, but she added she would have to ask the boys if they were in favor of having him join their family. He talked to them and told them how Molly felt.

"Does Molly want you to live with us?"

Molly said she thought it would be a good idea; if they didn't like Francisconia, they could always break it up.

The boys were quiet for a while and then Michael spoke up. "Listen, kids, it won't be bad to have another in our gang. Let's vote for it, and anyhow Aunt Molly wants him."

It was a bewildering situation. Francisconia wanted Molly. He was in love with her and if this was the only way he could have her it would have to do. Maybe later

he could persuade Molly to go through a marriage ceremony. But Molly never did. They lived together for thirty-
three years but never did go through a ceremony.

So, Francisconia came to live with the boys and Molly.
Now, the household consisted of Jews, Episcopalians, Baptists and a Catholic. Ultimately, Francisconia bought a
house large enough for the nine boys. It was a noisy household, but Molly loved the noise and tumult.

Francisconia would gaze at Molly with bewilderment
and think, "Who would have dreamed that at forty years
of age when I should have more sense, I would get involved
in such a situation." He would look at Molly, who now
wore four diamond engagement rings and introduced Francisconia as my husband to whom I am not married, ador-
ingly.

When three of the boys went off to war, he was as anx-
ious as Molly waiting for letters, and when they returned,
he gave a large sum to his church in thankfulness. It was
then that Molly reproached him.

"What about the temple? Isn't the Jewish God just as
responsible?"

Michael grinned at Francisconia. "I see she hasn't
changed, has she?"

When Sol's oldest son began to practice medicine, Molly
had a fit of crying.

"You should understand," she told her husband to whom
she was not married, "God is pleased with me."

"So what about getting married?"

"No, no, why should I tempt God? Let it be. You know
for me you are my life."

"And what about the boys?" Francisconia asked teas-
ingly.

"Ahhh," Molly sighed, "mine is a big heart."

Every one of the boys turned out to be good men and

successful men. On what would have been Molly's twenty-fifth wedding anniversary the boys gave her a wedding ring—one band with diamonds, one with rubies, and one with sapphires. "It's yours and our wedding, Molly. We love you."

Aunt Molly was the prototype of "My son, the doctor; my son, the professor; my son, the lawyer." The bond between the nine boys was remarkable. If one was in a jam and needed money, they all came to his rescue. When one was operated on and needed transfusions, all of them were at the hospital.

Michael was the first one to marry. His bride wanted a small wedding. Michael shook his head. "It can't be done. I have eight brothers."

"Isn't it enough if just your aunt Molly and Francisconia are present?"

"Never," said Michael. "It would break Molly's heart."

So Michael was married and his bride, to add to the confusion, was a Unitarian and all the boys were at the wedding along with Aunt Molly and her Francisconia.

With her great laugh, her warm heart, and tenderness to all humanity it was easy to be fond of Aunt Molly. The affection and regard between the nine of them was a tribute to the way Molly brought them up. She gave them and everyone who shared her life an example of what love can achieve. She lived for thirty-three years with the man she never married and never hid that fact from anyone. When Molly was dying, it was this man who sat beside her, holding her hand and comforting her. It was her nine sons who carried her to the bosom of the earth.

Everyone had warned Molly that the Italian would never stay without a legal marriage. The boys would be too much for him. But Francisconia was faithful to her all his life. Her death left a void that was never filled. The boys came to see him often and their children knew him as grandpa. Often he would reminisce about Molly's refusal to accept him until the boys gave their approval.

"I always hoped Molly would make it legal and marry me, but until the end she wouldn't. She was sure I would die if we were married."

The boys comforted him by telling him he couldn't have been more married even if there had been a ceremony. In the last years of his life he was lonely. He missed Molly, but the boys never neglected him. When his will was read it was a testimonial to Aunt Molly and his love and admiration for her. It read:

"My sons, all nine of them, need no money. I have given them an education, and they have filled me with pride. In memory of the sweet woman who was my wife in all but legal name, who took those nine boys who were not her own, who would not even accept me unless all nine approved of me, in her memory I bequeath my fortune to homeless, orphan children and hope that somewhere they, too, will find love as all of my nine sons did. I know they will not contest this will because I have talked it over with them and have asked the three eldest to be the executors of my earthly possessions."

That's why I revere my aunt Molly's memory, for if she was unconventional, her unorthodoxy was noble and good and her adopted family reflected her goodness.

Talk Shows and Hosts

I dislike being a guest on a talk show. My last experience with Jack Paar was enough to confirm that dislike. When Jack Paar was first on television he had the rare ability to discover personalities of individuality. They were on frequently and the nation grew to know them. Names that are now forgotten had instant acclaim after being on Jack Paar's show.

His was one of the first of the talk shows and an overwhelming success. He showed emotion, he was real, and people responded to his interest and feelings. The most enigmatic, unpredictable equation is what makes a television personality. There is no formula, no method by which one can test the quality which would assure one of being popular. It may be described as charisma, but what does that really mean?

Flip Wilson, Danny Kaye, Leonard Bernstein, Johnny Carson—each one is so different and yet each has appeal. Why does one newsman have a higher rating than another? Is it his smile, his voice, his earnestness, or his ability to transmit his humanness? No one knows what it is but everyone recognizes it when it is present.

Paar had it, but he certainly had none of it the night I was on his show. Sergio Franchi, a singer whose voice and sexy physique always bring him an ovation, was also on the program. Another guest was Uri Geller, the young Israeli psychic.

The interview with the Israeli was dismal and the interview with me was unbelievable. It ended abruptly with Mr. Paar rising from his seat with tears in his eyes. He left me there with Peggy Cass, who motioned me to remain seated and whispered, "He would have cried if he had remained."

I left the studio without seeing Jack or receiving an explanation from anyone for his peculiar behavior—a display of bad manners which left me bewildered. When I returned to Cleveland the next day I was pounced on at the station with "What did you do to Jack Paar?" Everyone presumed I had done or said something unkind to him. That really got to me. No one worried about me, only about Jack. We were besieged by telephone calls not only from local viewers but from other parts of the country with, "What happened? Why did Paar leave?"

That afternoon Paar called me from New York to give me an explanation. The fact that I came from Cleveland reminded him of his brother, who had died recently and is buried in Canton; his mother lives there; and he remembered his beginnings in the area. When he realized all that I was doing at my age and so on and so on . . . he ended his conversation with me by delivering the worst blow of all, "I only wish," he said, "that I were half the man you are." What could have been more deadly?

Some weeks later Uri Geller appeared on my show, and he is extraordinary. I've seen him bend an iron spike about one inch in diameter just by holding his hand an inch or two over it. Perhaps he changes the molecular structure of the metal. Perhaps his hand gives off some electrical current.

He also demonstrated his powers of telepathy. When he was out of the room I drew a figure on a sheet of paper and sealed it in five envelopes. Not only did he describe what I drew but pointed out that I hesitated because I thought of another drawing. A crystal ornament detached itself from a lamp while he was standing about six feet away, disregarding the law of gravity. It flew up and around Uri and then to the floor. This happened in my office, and there is no known way in which this crystal could become detached without someone using their fingers to do it. Since I was talking to Uri, who was at least six feet from the table on which the lamp stood, the whole episode is inexplicable. Uri told me that he doesn't know how he does this. Sometimes he feels that he is a computer being manipulated by aliens from other planets! Who knows? In any event, Mr. Paar created an atmosphere that made it difficult for him to function.

In a strange way Mike Douglas owes his fabulous success to the *One O'Clock Club*, which I hosted for a number of years. WEWS-TV was the first local station in the country to put on a live variety and talk show. We were on for an hour and a half. We ran away with the audience; the Westinghouse Broadcasting Company was determined to get the major part of that audience, and they did.

They hired Mike Douglas, who has warmth and charm. I've heard him entertain a huge audience at one of our Cleveland theaters—Musicarnival—for an hour and a half, singing to tumultuous applause. I've heard that the Westinghouse Broadcasting Company had allocated a large sum for his first year, which meant they paid for their talent, discouraging them from appearing on our show, since we did not pay our performers. Of course, that was in the

early days. It's different now. Later Bill Gordon took over
the show but, ultimately, I came back.

I've appeared on the Douglas show a number of times
and once Eva Gabor was on at the same time. Her English
vocabulary is somewhat limited and our dialogue was hilarious. I said that I loved sleeping with gardenias on my pil-
low. She exclaimed, "Gardenias! I love sleeping with my
husband!"

But I protested, "He couldn't smell as sweet as gardenias."

"Pooh," she retorted, "I perfume him before he comes to
bed."

Mike was convulsed with laughter. He is a comfortable
and encouraging host. The story is that when Mike Douglas
started, he had only two suits. Today he wears hundred-
dollar shoes.

Interviewing can be phony or honest, and it comes
through to the viewer. My purpose in an interview is to reveal the guest's opinions, prejudices, erudition, etc.

A panorama of individuals whose names are familiar to
most Americans have been my guests. Most of them I've
interviewed in WEWS-TV studios. Some, such as Willy
Brandt, Beatrice Lillie, Hitler, the governor of Cyprus,
Madam Chiang, Diego Rivera, the Shah of Iran, I've
crossed the seas to talk to.

Also, President Nixon; the late Harry Truman; Harry
Belafonte, a superb performer, whose confidence I had to
win; Margaret Mead, brilliant but supercilious; Helen
Hayes; Anita Loos, unassuming and modest; Senator Taft
and also his son, who now, like his father, is a senator; and
John Connally, who once a Democrat switched parties and
joined the Republican party—a change made after Watergate. It is ironic that a former Democrat may become the

banner bearer of the Republicans. Since there is very little difference in philosophy between the two major parties, his transfer to the Republican party must have been based on political expediency. He is both personable and likable and was a gracious and unassuming guest. He will have no difficulty with newsmen because he answers questions directly. Whether this will change if he should become President, no one knows.

But the presidency does strange things to men. Harry Truman rose to the office with nobility; the late FDR proved that an aristocrat could be moved to action by the agonies of a nation. In my interview with him he moved easily from political to personal questions. Unlike President Nixon, he did not avoid newsmen. He was gregarious enough to realize that a news conference is both dramatic and revealing, and a performance in which the President must use skill since the reporters direct questions with little delicacy when the purpose is to get information from the President.

Victor Borge, that incomparable, unique wit convulsed me with laughter most of the time. He is probably the most original wit of this generation. At one time my daughter had occasion to have dinner with him and his wife. A napkin was missing at my daughter's place so Borge tore his in half and gave one half to my daughter.

Holga Sandburg, the daughter of Carl Sandburg, who so magnificently enriched our literature, read some of the moving love poetry she has written. She dedicated it to her husband, Dr. Barney Crile, who challenged the accepted formula for the removal of breast cancer.

Another of my guests was Cyrus Eaton, at least twenty years ahead of his time when he urged recognition and trade with Russia. It took the Vietnamese war to bring the President and Kissinger to Mr. Eaton's point of view.

Recognition, I hope, does not mean approval of the Soviet's abrogation of the Russian citizens' freedom.

Julie Nixon Eisenhower and her young husband, David, were a delightful couple—so eager and interested in everything. Julie observed a picture of the late Duke of Windsor and myself in my office. She wanted me to tell her all about the duke, what he said to me, whether he talked about the duchess. However, when an interview with Julie Eisenhower was arranged when she came to Cleveland on September 9, 1973, she was anything but charming. She, apparently, didn't know about the interview and left abruptly. If whoever was in charge couldn't arrange a publicity tour for Julie Eisenhower, it's no wonder they messed up the presidential campaign.

Governor Rockefeller is a most likable human being. I told him I was surprised that he was elected governor. "Why?" he demanded, looking perplexed and I think slightly annoyed.

"Because," I answered, "I don't see how you can relate to the average American who has to worry about a job, about payments for the mortgage, the insurance, children's shoes, etc." "You," I told him, "have never known what it is to worry about money. Never once in your life! How can you comprehend the worries of the average voter?"

"That's not so," he answered. "I have some poor friends."

I doubt that. I understand that anyone with less than twenty million dollars is considered "poor rich." Perhaps he considers some in that category as his friends.

There is a fundamental difference in the outlook of a rich man as contrasted to that of the average man depending on a monthly salary—a sense of security, a freedom from anxiety. It colors the reactions and philosophy of the two groups. And significantly enough, very often it is the rich whose political philosophy is more liberal.

Unless our laws are changed, only rich men will occupy office. It took sixty million dollars to run President Nixon's campaign, which, of course, was ridiculous. Money wasn't needed to defeat Senator McGovern. He was too indecisive and bent too much with the wind of public opinion. Yet, ironically enough, he had all the instincts and convictions of a decent, honest liberal who was concerned about the people. I interviewed him and carried away the impression of a friendly, conscientious senator who was very aware of his responsibility as a member of the most powerful legis- lative group in the world.

Sixty million dollars to persuade the voters to elect Mr. Nixon is an unbelievable sum and in a way contributed to Watergate and all its duplicity and deception. Without that kind of money it would not have been possible for the Ehrlichmans and Haldemans and the retired policeman, Mr. Ulasewicz, and the Mitchells to have functioned.

The British limit the amount any man can spend or the amount any individual or corporation can contribute. Un- der their system no corporation or trade group or union can make the kind of contributions that would place the prime minister or any member of Parliament under obliga- tion. It is a rare individual who will contribute thousands of dollars to a campaign unless he or a corporation expects to receive favors from the candidate if he is elected. It's hu- man nature, and Watergate proved there are an awful lot of Watergates around.

I interviewed Walter Reuther, who was among the first of the labor leaders to add intellectuality to negotiations—

Labor has come a long way from the sixty-hour week in the steel mills at a fraction of what they are paid now. Reuther understood that unless the American worker was paid enough so that he could buy what he produces, no one would prosper in the United States. The consumer guarantees work; as long as the consumer, who is also the worker, is paid enough to buy the goods he produces, the magic circle of buying and selling remains unbroken and we continue to be an affluent society.

Pierre Rinfret has the talent for presenting the economic picture with humor and whimsicality. One must admit, however, with amazement and distress, that in spite of the hundreds of economists in the country our prices are swinging higher and higher up in the blue yonder and our dollar is being chiseled away before our very eyes. Our economy is gnawing away at the dollar in great bites!

The Shah of Iran is an effective ruler. Since his rule began, Iran has steadily progressed into the twentieth century. The standard of living is continuously rising. Illiteracy is being wiped out. He has manipulated the country's oil reserves into wealth and power for Iran. In a press conference he held in Tehran, which I attended, he was affable, friendly, and sure of himself. Presumably, being a Shah does engender self-confidence; there is no doubt that he is an enlightened ruler and politically aware of the role of oil in international affairs but he has never used oil as a political weapon. We were invited to the wedding reception where we were presented to the Shah's bride. It was a Moslem wedding but the queen wore a Dior gown.

It must have been quite a sight some years later when the Shah and President Kennedy stood at the bottom of the stairway in the White House and watched the queen, magnificently arrayed in fabulous jewels and a diadem, and Jacqueline Kennedy, in her elegant gown with but one jewel for adornment, descending the stairway. Little did any of the actors in this festive occasion dream that not too many years later would find Jacqueline Kennedy a widow and destined to become the wife of one of the richest men in the world, with jewels that must surely rival the queen of Iran.

James Reston is a reasonable, unassuming man, indubitably the most respected journalist in the country. If all records of our time were destroyed except for his commentaries, we would have the history of our generation. A half-hour interview with him was like an excursion into the brain of a modern man—wise and aware and courageous. I noticed that he had the attention of the floormen and engineers in the dialogue between us. He is a mature, moral American with a fine mind and the ability to express in written words the concepts of a reflective man. It is one of the advantages of my position constantly to meet and enjoy rare minds, some iconoclastic, some profound, some noble. It's been a postgraduate course of no mean significance.

Magic and magicians have fascinated people throughout the ages. The ancient priests in Egyptian and Babylonian times used magic to instill awe in the people. Milbourne Christopher is a renowned magician who has written a book titled *History of Magic*. When I interviewed him, I asked him if magic is based on illusion.

"Completely," he answered. "There is nothing supernatural involved."

He is also skeptical about mediums and communications with the dead, levitation, and fortunetellers. He said "yes" when I asked him if he could perform the same tricks as Houdini did, such as managing to emerge from a strongbox that had been locked, wrapped in iron chains, and lowered into the waters of a lake. But Mr. Christopher added that he was not as good a performer as Houdini, who added drama to his magic. Houdini was, Mr. Christopher said, without doubt the greatest magician in recorded history.

Mr. Christopher told me about a fascinating episode. In Cuba a winning lottery number was to be announced; Mr. Christopher journeyed to Cuba, gave the officials there a sealed envelope containing a number which he said would be found to be the winning number. The envelope was placed in a bank vault and guarded. After the winning number was announced, the envelope was opened and it contained, as Mr. Christopher said it would, the winning number.

"How did you know that?" I asked. Obviously, he wouldn't tell me, but to me it seemed like magic.

I also interviewed Colonel Edwin Aldrin, Jr., who stepped on the moon immediately after Neil Armstrong. The world watched and it was the first time in millenniums of time, the first time that any creature left this planet, this earth, and the thin layer of oxygen upon which our living depends. Where else in the universe was a signal sounded that man had left his earth-bound home and started his journey into space? What sensation overwhelmed these two? Colonel Aldrin, Jr., said they were so busy executing the details of their exploration of the moon that they had no time to think of their startling experience. This is a man with a high intelligence and the courage to describe his depressions, which he fought so valiantly. Whether his chromosomes and genes are responsible for the depressions or whether the cause was the tremendous emotional upheaval he endured becoming a world-famous hero and having a love affair with a woman who was not his wife, is not certain. What is certain is that he went through agony. There are many individuals who have to fight depressions that come and then disappear. I myself very frequently feel depressed on Sundays, probably because I don't have as much to do as on all other days. I was very moved by the colonel's candor. To be a world hero must make it difficult to adjust to a mere pedestrian existence. But forever he will be marked with a unique and awe-inspiring achievement.

Billy Graham's personality and interest are geared to the emotionally religious. He is impressive, handsome, friendly, with great personal charm. He is a fundamentalist and in an expanding universe he still finds the literal acceptance of the Bible reasonable. In many ways he is a great performer, magnetizing his audience.

Elliot Janeway has a facile mind but bad manners in a panel discussion. He was rude to one of the most brilliant and original minds of any man I have met—Samuel Henry Miller, whose brilliance is only equaled by his wisdom and whose arresting face carries a torch of sadness, as though he knew man's vulnerability to the pursuit of power and money no matter what the price.

Many of my guests have written books on topics of general or national interest; some of them are novelists.

Jacqueline Susann swept the country like a meteor for she is a great raconteur. She can tell a story and her dialogue is very modern and superb. She is a product of her time and reflects our mores. If Balzac had been writing in the twentieth century, his plots, too, would have reflected this period, which emphasizes vulgarities, obscenities, deviates, and drugs.

Carl Stokes, mayor of Cleveland for four years, has more charm than a dozen people put together. I once interviewed Carl, his brother, Louis Stokes, and his mother. It was for me a moving experience. His mother had been a cleaning woman, cleaning homes and apartments of the affluent, frequently bringing clothes back to the boys given to her by some of the families she worked for. She is a sweet, unpretentious woman. It must have been quite an experience for her to be black and poor, to work as a cleaning woman, and to see both her sons not only succeed but reach places of eminence. It would be a Horatio Alger story in any case, but to be black and achieve this was a greater victory—a victory in the face of almost unsurpass-able odds. I interviewed Carl when his book came out and during the course of our talk, germane to something he said, I countered by saying, "You really don't like whites."

He grinned and answered, "Oh, some of my best friends are white."

I looked at him reproachfully and said, "That's not worthy of you."

Charles Ashman wrote a book about Kissinger and also *The Best Judges Money Can Buy*. It was on my show that his present sponsors heard him and offered him a talk show. He had never been on TV but they were taken with his outgoing personality, a quality which is very engaging. He is talkative and articulate. The silent type is not necessarily deep. Mostly they are silent because they have nothing to say. I infinitely prefer the articulate type. Imagine having to spend an evening with the silent type. In any event, they signed Mr. Ashman and he has now twenty-eight sta-tions. I told him he really should pay me a percentage but he very gallantly settled with roses. And he is very good as a host of a talk show. The popularity of talk shows reveals the hunger people have to hear what other people think and how they feel. To be able to express opinions and to describe emotions is a gift—uniquely man's. An eloquent speaker literally can almost lift an audience to its feet. Until we use words we are strangers to each other. The viewers of the talk shows admire honesty and candor. To have a guest honest in his answers, to have the courage to reveal himself is a refreshing experience for the viewer.

Philip Stern, who wrote of *The Rape of the Taxpayer*, is a delightful chap. We had quite a chat and he rather shyly asked if I had time to have lunch. I had asked him earlier how long it took to do the research and then write the

book. He told me several months. I presumed that he had
no income during these months and not wanting to expose
him to the extra expense of paying for my lunch I said I
was too busy to take the time. I only discovered later that
this unassuming erudite young man could pay for my lunch
a hundred times without any pain because he was the
grandson of General Robert E. Wood, the long-time head
of Sears, Roebuck.

Erich Segal's book, *Love Story*, swept the country. He
appeared on my show before any others, and I told him
then that he had a winner. The country was fed up with
abnormal beings and perverts; an honest, normal love story
was a relief. The movie was refreshing compared to *Last
Tango in Paris*, where Marlon Brando, a superb actor, is so
unspeakably wicked and brutal. Significantly enough, *Love
Story* was a smashing success. *Tango* is really a bore, in
spite of some of the rave reviews by critics so sophisticated
that only the odd and ugly move them to praise.

There is very little noble writing today, no fine novels
such as *God Is an Englishman* or *Horseman Riding By*,
by R. F. Delderfield, John Williams' *Augusta* or Petrakis'
In the Land of Morning, Don Robertson's *Paradise Falls*.
Clinical obsessions with ugliness, brutality, violence, per-
version, characters without manners, and orgasms are de-
picted in the theater; males embracing each other, copulating to the sound of music, urinating on the stage, as in
Picasso's *Le Désir Attrapé par la Queue*, Genet's *The Balcony*, where a scene is acted out showing one of the characters castrating himself.

Obviously, people do urinate and, admittedly, castration
is not an everyday occurrence, but should not literature
and the theater be dedicated to emphasizing the good, the
sweet, the tender in life, not the ugly and the brutal?

Great literature has ennobled men. It reveals the agonies
of all lives in their endeavor to discipline themselves into

creatures above brutal and cruel instincts. Life without discipline—inner discipline—results in a formless ignoble individual, forever at the mercy of his animalistic instincts.

Why should not both literature and the novel exalt man? Good manners in outward conduct are the expression of considerate manners of the inner being. Why should the modern novel depict only the perverted, the sick? Isn't normal sex beautiful enough? For how much longer will the contemporary novel be spiritually sterile?

I interviewed David Frost in a limousine riding to the airport with our cameraman hunched on the front seat. It was a unique experience and I suspect Mr. Frost thought it was wild, mad, and as funny as I did. I asked him how it felt to be so successful. He had always been happy, he said. He had a secure and happy childhood, which certainly enables one to reach a secure and neurosis-free maturity.

Sally Rand, famous for her fan dance, was going to college when I interviewed her and was sewing to entertain herself. She may have been sexy on the stage but no one could have been more matter-of-fact and pleasant, without anything stagey about her. After the interview a viewer sent me two enormous ostrich fans, each one opening at least five feet in width and six feet high. Unfortunately, I never had occasion to use them as Sally did.

Gypsy Rose Lee, the most sophisticated of the stripteasers, was aghast that I allowed myself to be televised without a silk screen to hide any wrinkles or other signs of age.

"That's ridiculous," she told me; "I wouldn't allow them to televise me so brutally." Fortunately for me my vanity takes a different form. I see no reason why I should hide my age. My friends don't agree with me. They tell me that we live in a period where age is a handicap and all attention is turned on youth. This was the reason they say they would never tell their age.

Some years after the interview I happened to meet Gypsy Rose Lee on the Riviera. She was having coffee on the terrace of her hotel. She said, "Join me in a cup of coffee," which I did. She never asked how I happened to be there or wasn't it strange that we should meet there. She simply proceeded as though it were the most natural thing in the world for me to bump into her in France. I never saw her again. She died some years later of cancer. She was married a number of times. Her marriages never worked out, she said, because she was too efficient, not helpless enough, not dependent enough. "What I need to develop is helplessness," she told me.

I've interviewed a number of stripteasers, headliners at the burlesque theater. Each one had a different gimmick. Some were college graduates and quite freely said that their reason for appearing in burlesque was the pay. Where else, they asked me, could they earn one thousand dollars and even two thousand dollars a week? With the complete freedom accorded to sex and pornography, burlesque houses now have little to offer. Very little is hidden in the mini-skirt and bikini, which can be viewed at any beach free. They've killed the burlesque houses where the stripteaser with her thirty seconds of revealed nudity was the feature act. Why pay three dollars to see a stripteaser when revealed flesh stares one in the face everywhere? The Romans at least wore a toga over their briefs, which were the same length as the mini-dress.

We killed romance with sexual freedom. A woman no longer has to develop the fine art of coquetry nor the male, the art of wooing. When I was in my early teens, I used to gobble up novels. They became my dream world, particularly at the point where the hero took the heroine in his arms and drew her to him.

The Supreme Court's decision, that pornography is a

local responsibility, represents some dangers, for the decision will, undoubtedly, create chaos. There is always the danger that the sex vigilantes will impose their code on everyone else. The truth, however, is that sexual lawlessness and obscenity in the theater, in books, and in magazines have become excessive. Sex is a private matter and as long as it is private, it surely is not any government agency's business. To make it illegal to sell a book that is pronounced pornography by some local officer but which in other areas is considered great writing may become unadorned bigotry and has no place in modern society.

I must confess it outrages me to hear scatological words used so freely in conversation to prove that "I am with it." I should not be obliged to listen to the use of words which should be confined to latrines.

In my years as an interviewer I've talked to literally thousands of generous, heroic, principled, warm men and women. Since appearing with me in an interview, Bing Crosby's wife still sends me a Christmas card every year. Erma Bombeck has a wonderful, whimsical sense of humor. The whole country is obsessed with diets and how to stay thin and I have talked with a number of diet specialists. Melina Mercouri is a fine actress and completely dedicated to the cause of freedom for Greece. There is something magnificent about such dedication and uncompromising repudiation of a government that is not a democracy. Eartha Kitt exuded sex appeal. Marian Anderson, in addition to an unforgettable voice, has more dignity than any other person I've ever interviewed. Ed Sullivan is a fortunate man who took what destiny gave him and brought pleasure to millions of people. And like all really successful people he was modest and friendly. Sybil Leek insists she is a witch (a good one) and has made a lucrative career of it.

Teddy Kollek, the urbane and courageous mayor of Jerusalem, is a courageous man. During the Six Day War he rode through the streets of his city unmindful of the shells and gunfire. Daniel Ellsberg, whose court case will remain one of the most dramatic in our legal history, was on my show. As a result of Watergate his story has had a dramatic ending and proved once more that the dissidents, those who put their beliefs into action, are the real molders and makers of man's history. Vivian Kellems also defied the government. She refused to withold income tax from her employees' pay. In true Yankee tradition she fought to sustain her convictions but lost her fight in the courts. I found Jimmy Hoffa a man with great personal charm and a most persuasive manner. Sir Edmund Hillary was a guest; he had to scale Mount Everest because it was there.

Bob Hope, Dionne Warwicke, Liberace, Eva Gabor, Zsa Zsa Gabor, and Helen Keller, who filled me with awe and even reverence. What can one say about a brain that transcended the limitation of a body without sight or the ability to hear and yet could comprehend abstract ideas?

Scientists, oil magnates, heroic firemen and policemen, governors and senators, economists, nuns and priests, rabbis, circus performers, an endless array—literally thousands have appeared on my show. We once tried to add up the number and gave it up after we reached ten thousand. How many gifted, how many brainy, how many compassionate, how many ambitious, how many great performers I have sat with and talked to. A galaxy of stars and I have taken whatever wisdom and erudition they have offered. The human animal is amazing—the challenge to achieve constantly animates him.

A Tragic Story

As I look back at some of my adventures, I feel an ache for the yesterdays that can never come back. So many whom I have loved, so many with whom I laughed, and so many over whom I have shed tears. One's life is a mosaic made up of many pieces, some brilliant in color, some subdued, some dramatic, and some gray and somber. We are like freight trains. Each year adds to our memories and the sweetest are often in the cars far back.

What would one give, what ransom, what payment to bring back a day, to live over a burnished hour, to hear a voice, to touch a hand, to renew a vow of love forever and ever gone? Are we only shadows that flee across the stream of time? Does time somewhere in the universe perpetuate our days of living? Perhaps the remembering and the re-telling of a tale "twice told" gives it some perpetuity, some immortality.

Before the Second World War, Roseka, my close girl-hood friend with whom I took many trips (as those of you who read my book, *I Laughed, I Loved, I Cried*, will re-call), and I boarded an export boat from Germany bound

for the Middle East on a night of warmth and perfume
covered by a sky of velvet and purple. The export boats
were broad-beamed and were very steady and comfortable, even for someone like myself, who can turn green
with seasickness merely at the sight of a steamship ticket.
They were designed so that four rooms surrounded a private deck, which was quite luxurious, for it meant that if
one wanted to sit out on deck it wasn't necessary, as is
customary, to go on the main deck.

The occupants of the four cabins generally become
pretty well acquainted. The occupant of one of the cabins
was a man with a dark mustache, obviously very reserved,
and always with a book in his hand, reading. I noted that
once the book was in French, at another time it was in
German, and once in Italian. I wondered who he was.
Roseka and I conjectured about him.

"I'll bet he is a stuffy Frenchman."

"No," I said, "I think he is a pompous German or maybe
he is just a lecherous Italian."

"What if he were none of those?"

"What difference does it make?"

"Well," she answered, "I was about to engage in a little
bet. I bet you two dollars he's a Frenchman."

"Even if I bet that he isn't, what good would it do you,
because how are we going to find out?"

"By a very difficult and complicated method," said
Roseka. "I'm just going to ask him."

"Do you mean to tell me that you are rude enough to
go up to the man and question him?"

"Certainly," she said, "I've been looking for some identification but since he has never said anything I can't figure
him out. He nods his head good morning, but how can
you tell the difference between an English, a German, or
a French nod!"

"Do you have to know? He doesn't look very interesting to me."

Roseka said plaintively, "I've surveyed the rest of the passengers and the result is doleful. He's about as promising as any in looks. He has a crisp, black mustache."

"Well, count me out," I said. "I can't abide mustaches. So he is all yours. I'm not the least bit interested."

"But you have to take the bet," said Roseka.

"Why?"

"So I can have an excuse for asking."

"All right, I'll bet the opposite of your bet, whatever it is, but not two dollars. One dollar is as high as I will go."

A few minutes after this animated and important conversation, the man with the mustache came strolling onto the deck, nodded, and didn't utter a word. I thought that Roseka would be snubbed by this and walk away, but she was on the spot, for she knew I was watching her and enjoying her embarrassment.

"Excuse me," she said, "I'm an American and I wonder if you would tell me whether you are French or German or Italian."

He smiled and answered in a cultured English voice, "Why should I?"

"Because I have a bet on."

I spoke up. "Don't you tell her or I'll lose a dollar."

He threw back his head and laughed. "I certainly don't want you to lose any money on me, but you are both wrong! I'm neither French nor Italian nor German."

Simultaneously, we both cried, "English!"

"Not so fast." He was, apparently, enjoying the encounter and said, "You'd better cancel your bet, because both of you will lose."

"Ah," said Roseka, "you were a foundling and were

brought up by an English butler who taught you how to speak the English way!"

"Go on," he said. "What else have you figured out?"

"Oh, well," answered Roseka, "then the master of the home adopted you and left you his fortune."

"How charming," he exclaimed, "but what would my own parents say about this?"

He was delightful and, though inclined to be rather solemn, his erudition was impressive. He spoke a number of languages and could quote from the literature of various nationalities. He completely fascinated me with his limitless knowledge and his quiet, reserved manner. We discovered that he was of English descent, but had been born in Bangkok, where he lived, and to where he was returning. He had been in Germany on business. His family, we learned, represented some insurance as well as automobile interests. He was very sober and grim when he told me that he was sure there was another war coming.

"This man Hitler," he said, "is working himself up into a frenzy or into a hysteria and only one thing will satisfy him and that is war. He is filled with the romantic nonsense of Valhalla and German superiority. Not since the degenerate days of the Roman emperors Nero and Caligula has the world seen anything like this man and the holocaust that he is likely to cause." "England," he continued, "was particularly vulnerable because of the German Luftwaffe."

No man could have foreseen the remarkable valor of the English and the strange German paralysis in not crossing its army over to England after Dunkirk. But those tragic events were still in the future. We were on a long voyage and the companionship of the stranger, whose name we learned was Phillip K., helped while away the hours.

He had his place changed from the captain's table to ours

and the noon and dinner hours were gay and laughing affairs. Roseka amused Phillip.

"Are all American women like her?"

"Heavens, no!" I assured him. "In every nation there is only one such wild and unpredictable female."

Roseka had engaged in a flirtation with a dark-eyed, suave South American who could tango with verve and dash, so that Phillip and I found ourselves alone a good part of the time. We walked on deck, we played deck tennis, we swam, and we talked. As we approached Alexandria, he suggested that I have lunch with him there, for he was leaving the boat at the Alexandrian port.

The boat docked at Alexandria and I accepted his invitation to lunch, since we were informed by the purser that the boat would have a three-hour layover. I had never been in Alexandria before and I was curious to see it.

This was the city that was established by Alexander the Great when he crossed the Alps and made himself conqueror of the known world at that time. It was in this city, named for him, that his body was placed in a golden sarcophagus, which was later looted.

Egypt has heard the tread of conquering armies many times. We Americans are completely free of any such historic memories and that fact must account in great measure for our dauntlessness and assurance that we can accomplish anything.

We dined leisurely and drove up the Cornish drive and returned to find, to my dismay and distress, that the boat had left. Apparently, we had either misunderstood or been given the wrong information. There would not be another boat leaving for five days. I was filled with consternation.

Phillip said, "There is no use in bewailing the matter. It is my fault. I should have checked more carefully. Perhaps there is a boat that will take you to England and you can then transfer to an export steamer."

After we figured that one out, it was obvious that I would arrive home just as fast as if I waited the five days.

"What will I do? I have no clothes with me."

"That is not a matter of worry," he answered. "In twenty-four hours you will have a complete outfit."

Then Phillip made a suggestion. "Since you will have five days, why don't you fly to Bangkok with me? You have never been there, and I should like to show you the country. It is rich in legend and lore."

I was disconsolate. It was such an absurd thing to have allowed to happen. Fortunately, I didn't have any engagement in the States which I had to keep.

"What will I do about clothes?"

"Don't worry about that. It can easily be arranged as soon as we arrive in Bangkok."

I decided I might as well be philosophical about the whole episode and at least see Siam. So we flew over to Bangkok and Phillip arranged rooms for me at the hotel and told me that my wardrobe would be taken care of immediately. While waiting, I sent a cable home and one to Roseka, on the ship. I could imagine how her eyebrows went up. I also knew I would have quite a time persuading her to believe that the whole thing was a ridiculous blunder.

In a short while, a tailor, a dressmaker, and a shoeman appeared and it is a fact that in twenty-four hours I had two suits, three dresses, two negligées, and petticoats, and three pairs of shoes, all perfectly fitted. I had begun to be philosophic about the delay and the complete wardrobe certainly helped to reconcile me to the wait. When the costumes had been delivered, another messenger arrived with a velvet box, and in the box was a jeweled wristwatch, with a note saying, "Please accept this to atone in some small measure for the delay. And now you can watch the time." Every day flowers were delivered to my suite.

Since Phillip was busy part of the day, I engaged a guide to take me around. Bangkok, Venice of the East, is no Venice. It is true the city is built on canals and on the river but the houses are wooden and most of them stand on stilts. It has none of the ineffable, unbelievable beauty of Venice, where so long ago men wrought a city of such incomparable loveliness that after centuries men continue to go there to behold its beauty and marvel that so much harmony could be wrought out of stone.

Because it's strange to my ears I find oriental music thin and reedy. I am attuned to, and comfortable with, the sonorous majesty of Western music, which derived from the liturgical music of the church. The great chants of the Jewish ritual were taken up by the Catholic churches and the result is the symphonic music of the West, which found its first great expression in Bach.

The temples in Bangkok are ornate, inlaid with jade and gold—tier upon tier rising up to hundreds of feet. They are neither Gothic nor Greek and didn't command my attention, except by their size and inlays of gold and jewels. In Gothic churches, men aspired to soar to the heavens. In Greek architecture, men aspired to a harmony and serenity. Buddhist temples doubtless have the same aspirations but to my eye they don't seem to particularly belong to the land. East and West, in every area of life, seem very different.

The waters of the rivers are used for bathing, for washing clothes, for brushing teeth. There is plenty of dysentery and intestinal infections. The infants that survive, apparently, build up an immunity against bacterial infections, but there is no famine here nor are there beggars. And, if the waters of the rivers and canals are dirty, they are at the same time picturesque-looking. The early morning with boatloads of fruit and vegetables converging on the market-place in a bend in the river is a painter's delight with its variegated colors.

The floating market is colorful and animated and gay. Boats of all sizes, loaded with fruits, meats, vegetables, dishes, with material for dresses, boats delivering milk, joined the procession. Anything that could be purchased in a store was to be found on the boats. There was a lively exchange of conversation, with laughter and sunshine. Boats with the postman delivering mail, stopping to chat, children being rowed to school. Siam had not only enough food for herself, but plenty to export and rice was being transported from the small boats to the ocean-going freighters. There was none of the horrifying poverty that one saw in India for example.

My guide told me that the best time to see the boats on the canals, which they call "klongs," was in October, for then a great festival takes place. The king leads a procession down the river to the Temple of Dawn. It is at this time that he presents new robes to the priest, the saffron-colored ones that they wear with their heads shaved. The king's regal-looking boat is over a hundred and fifty feet long and the legend is that it is carved from one single tree. At least, it is long enough to necessitate over a half a hundred rowers.

The sun is hot, it is scorching, but the king doesn't have to worry about a little thing like that, for he sits in a golden pavilion. He is accompanied by forty or fifty boats that take part in the procession. The mosquitoes are vicious—how they keep these insects away from his royal presence has not been revealed. It would be unseemly for his royal majesty to have to scratch like the rest of us commoners.

My guide was six-feet-three with shiny eyes and teeth—

a handsome male. Married, of course. They always are, if
they are good-looking! He had five children. But in the
course of the conversation he told me that he was not a
ripe man. I would have thought that anyone with five
children was pretty ripe.

"What do you mean," I demanded, "that you are not a
ripe man?"

"I am a Buddhist," he explained, "and no Buddhist is
truly a ripe man, a mature man, until he has spent some time
wearing the saffron robe of the monk with shaved head,
living only on what alms he may receive from the pious."

There is profound wisdom in this philosophy, for only
if you yourself have lived on the wrong side of the railroad track can you understand the emotions and the frustrations of the poor, the humble, and the downtrodden.

"My father asks me in every letter I receive from him
when I will spend my time as a monk."

"Why haven't you?" I asked.

"Oh, I'm too busy making money."

I thought he must be earning thousands of dollars when
I heard his answer. But he proceeded to tell me that he
made a hundred dollars a month, had five children and two
servants, and saved fifty dollars a month! So, go to Bangkok and live without worry on your Social Security and,
if you should have two hundred a month, you could live
regally—that is, if you can stand the heat!

I received a note from Phillip's mother inviting me to
have lunch with them. A car was sent to bring me to their
home and it was obvious that these were people of enormous wealth, for the car drove at least a half mile through
the private grounds surrounding the house, which was built
according to the architecture of the country. I was greeted
at the door by Phillip and his mother, a quiet, unassum-

ing-looking woman with a sweet smile, unostentatiously dressed.

I wondered whether Phillip was married or a bachelor. I had never asked him, and the matter had never come up in conversation. His father was an Englishman, but his mother, obviously, was Siamese. The house was sumptuously furnished with magnificent hangings to keep the sun out; great fans hidden by flowers and statuary kept the air moving. The dining room was regal in its appointments and there were four butlers for five guests. In addition to myself, there were two male guests, business associates of Phillip's father. The conversation was bright and sprightly and if I felt any embarrassment when I arrived, it was quickly dissipated, for Phillip's father told the guests of how I had been stranded and said that he suspected his son of some duplicity in this matter, as it was the only time he had known him to make a mistake about departure time. The easy way in which they joked about it made it pleasant for me, and his father suggested that, since I was there, I might as well see the countryside, and arrangements were made for a number of excursions.

The fourth day arrived and the next day meant I would be leaving. That afternoon Phillip rang me and asked if he could pick me up by two o'clock. Since I was with him every day, this was routine, but when we were in the car Phillip said, "I have not spoken of my wife, but today I have arranged to have you meet her."

I was silenced. I could have said, "You haven't acted as though you had a wife, and why haven't you mentioned her before?" But pride kept me from my comment.

However, Phillip was a perceptive man. He leaned over and touched my hand. "I think," he said, "you will understand."

I was silent until we reached his home. A nurse was at the bottom of the stairs and Phillip said, "How is she?"

"Waiting to see you, sir."

I walked up the great stairway and followed Phillip into the room. I held my breath, for if ever I had imagined what Sleeping Beauty of the fairy tale looked like, here was the vision of her lying as though in dreamless slumber, black hair surrounding her head, closed eyes fringed with long lashes, and a flush to her cheeks. I thought she looked like an angel. But my eye also caught an oxygen tent and Phillip said, "Polio."

She could not move anything except her head. Her hands, which lay upon the sheets, were as white and soft as though they were made of velvet. The flush, I was sure, was rouge which the nurse had placed upon her cheeks.

She smiled as Phillip called to her, "Grace, this is the American girl I told you about."

She opened her eyes. "How do you do?" she said. "Phillip told me about you and I hope you are not having too bad a time waiting for your boat. Also, I am glad that Phillip is having a little recreation, for he tells me you are very clever and keep him laughing a good part of the time."

I had no clever answers. I was simply numbed with horror that so beautiful a creature should be condemned to this kind of torture.

We stayed for about fifteen minutes and then the nurse suggested that we leave. I said "good-by," telling her that I would not see her again as my boat was leaving the next day.

"Well," she answered with a smile, "don't trust Phillip to get you there on time."

Phillip leaned down and kissed her forehead and we left.

I was absolutely stricken with grief for Phillip and I

couldn't talk. It was not until we returned to the hotel that I broke the silence by saying, "Why didn't you tell me, Phillip?"

"I don't know why," he answered. "I just couldn't. I felt that if you met her, you would understand. We were married five years ago and after three months she became ill with polio and this is the result as you saw it today. The nurse wanted us to leave because she spends most of her time in the oxygen tent. I loved her very much, but death would be easier than to see her this way. Now you know why I have not told you how I feel about you. For I have nothing to offer you. I could ask you to be my mistress, but even if you should acquiesce to such a suggestion, you would hate me afterwards, for that position is an ignominious one for a proud woman. I needn't tell you that I am loath to see you go. Meeting you has been the only happy or gay thing that has occurred since Grace was stricken, and it will be lonely again when you leave."

I looked at Phillip. A world divided us, a world of space as well as a world of emotion. What could I say to this brilliant man with a towering intellect, and yet so forlorn? He had wealth, position, prestige, the rich life of an intellectual, but was doomed not only to loneliness but sadness.

I leaned over and slipped both my hands in his. "Phillip, Phillip," I said, "even if my heart were breaking at leaving you, what can I say? What can I do? I, too, have commitments which I will not desert. My life does not belong here, but I will leave part of my heart with you, for I am as close to loving you as I dare."

And I began to weep. Where there might have been the splendor of great love, there was only sadness and tears.

His mother and father came with him to see me off, so I was spared a heartbreaking scene of good-by.

The next year I came to Budapest and Phillip arranged

to come down for a couple of days. My room was filled with white flowers when I checked in the hotel, and when I woke there was a gypsy band underneath my balcony serenading me. Around noon Phillip arrived and I met him at the station. We spent two days wandering through the exotic city. We sat at cafés and listened to the gypsy bands. We went to Margarhita Island and picnicked there on the green lawn with a box lunch packed by the hotel. We dined under the starlight on the banks of the river. At night we were lovers.

He told me more of his life. His father was a rich aristocrat and his mother a Siamese princess; he had been sent away to school in England from the age of twelve; he had been lonely and homesick. He told me of his marriage to the beautiful and dying Grace. He hardly had time to learn to love her when this dread disease struck, the terrifying tragedy that had doomed her, and he told me how, as a result of this, he had become lonelier; and of his pain at seeing her suffer and knowing that only death would release her. He told me, too, how refreshing Roseka and my banter on the boat had been and how he treasured the hours and how he would remember these.

He had only two and a half days with me. The last hour he took me to an art studio and there bought two paintings—one an evening scene and the other a morning scene.

"You," he said, "are to have the morning scene. I will have the night scene and, perhaps, when you look at the picture you will think of me."

"I will remember you always, Phillip, and though our time together has been so brief, its intensity has already marked my heart. I will not forget you, Phillip. Your memory will stay very dear to me."

"My dear, my dear," he answered, "my might-have-been

love. When I leave, I will just put you in a cab and no
good-bys. I could not endure it."

So, he left me and I never saw Phillip again, for the war
came and he joined the British Army. I was sure that he
would, for he had spoken to me frequently of his horror
of Hitler, who was determined to conquer England.

"What will you do," I had asked him, "if the war should
break out?"

"I will join the British Army, for my ancestors came
from England and I owe something to my heritage."

He was, of course, truly chivalrous and hundreds of
thousands like him gave their lives to save England and all
that she stood for.

Did Phillip have a premonition when he gave me the
sunrise canvas and kept the sunset for himself? Did he
divine that sunset would come early for him—death in the
waters of the Atlantic in a flaming, plunging plane. A piece
of my heart went down with him.

Years later I went back to Bangkok. I called on Phillip's
mother, who remembered me in a vague way. Grace,
Phillip's mother told me, was dead. In the sitting room
where Phillip's mother received me, there was a portrait
of Phillip. I gazed at it for a long time trying to capture
the quality which was so uniquely his, but it was of no
avail. His mother, seeing me gazing at the portrait said,
"Would you like a photograph of it?" I shook my head. It
was easier not to have a picture of him. Phillip no longer
belonged to the living, only to my memory.

In a German Garden

Several years ago the German government invited me to go to Germany as their guest. The invitation was conveyed to me by the German consul, Irene Meyers, a superior official and a delightful human being. They would arrange any interview I desired. When the publishers of Albert Speer's book learned that I was thinking of going to Germany, they phoned to say that they would arrange an interview for me with Speer. Speer, you will recall, was the munition czar under Hitler and was the only Nazi at Nuremberg who said, "I am guilty." He was convicted and sentenced to twenty years. While in jail he began writing and finished his book after he was released. He seems to have been the only literate Nazi around Hitler and his book will indubitably remain source material for historians in the future.

Accordingly, I flew to Munich and from there phoned Herr Speer, who lives in the lovely city of Heidelberg, made so famous by the light opera *The Student Prince*. He suggested that I fly to Heidelberg and have lunch with him. This was about ten-thirty in the morning. I accepted, flew over, and an hour later I met Speer. Speer's home was several miles from the airport and I drove through hills covered with trees and old, interesting houses. When I arrived at the Speer home, a house which had been built seventy years ago by his father, I was ushered into the garden. Through all the days of my life I will remember this. It was a day in September when the sun feels like a warm caress on one's face. Roses were blooming, off in the distance I could hear a bird singing, and occasionally a butterfly would cross my vision. It was a scene of utter tranquility. Dear God, I thought, how can this be? Three decades before the world had rocked with a catastrophic war and now it was as though it had never happened. A world was almost destroyed, and I was waiting for one of the men who had plotted to vanquish and take over Europe.

When Speer came out to greet me, a man of great charm and presence, I said to him "Herr Speer, I must tell you at once that the ghosts of millions of dead, wounded, imprisoned, and displaced people stand between you and me." He nodded gravely and in a resigned manner. He is a cultivated man, reasonable, courteous, and good-looking. How was it possible that he had been part of the unbelievable design that had drenched the world with blood? All the perfumes of Arabia will not wipe out this crime. Yet, there he stood, once Hitler's czar of all the industrial power of Germany transferred into a war engine.

"Tell me," I asked him, "why did you plead guilty?"

"Because I was guilty," he answered. "I closed my eyes to what was happening because my ambition was so great. Hitler gave me the fulfillment of an architect's dream, carte blanche to rebuild Berlin as I desired. Who would not have paid almost any price for such an opportunity? Then the war came and my dream for a new Berlin was shoved aside and Hitler appointed me czar of all German industries to produce armaments. By then I was too involved to withdraw."

"But, Herr Speer," I asked, "couldn't you smell the dead flesh in the gas chamber, couldn't you hear the cry of little children, didn't you know that behind the trim, landscaped concentration camps, children were being held naked in their mothers' arms, their clothes neatly piled in great stacks, and shoved into gas chambers? Didn't you realize that you were using slave labor in your factories pouring out instruments of destruction?"

"No," he said. "I closed my eyes to all of what was happening because it was too late. I had no choice or I would have also been a victim, too, for Hitler was irrational."

He told me of the last days of Hitler's life. In the bunker with Hitler was Eva Braun, his mistress of many years. Hitler urged her to leave the bunker while there was still time; she refused and it was here in the bunker that Hitler married her. His wedding gift to her was a suicide pact. Did ever the world record a marriage such as this? Above the bunker could be heard the thunder of the Russian Army, approaching and encircling Berlin while Hitler and his mistress were declared man and wife. Here Hitler gave his last commands. Hitler, before whose armies one nation after another has fallen like pins in a bowling alley. Now his army was encircled by the Allied armies. In a frenzy, Hitler had ordered all of Germany to be destroyed. It did not deserve to survive. "Let all go down into the flames of defeat, let there be a Götterdämmerung," he thundered. From this bunker beneath the city of Berlin, Hitler ordered that all of Germany be destroyed, factories bombed, cities destroyed, Germans to die as Hitler himself, all to be consumed by the flames of destruction. A funeral pyre of all of Germany for Hitler, Germany's idol, Hitler, the con-

queror! It was then that Speer knew Hitler had to be killed.
He and a few others planned to do away with Hitler; but
they were too late. Hitler, determined never to be taken
by the allies, committed suicide.

On his wedding day there was a breakfast attended by
everyone in the bunker, champagne was served and toasts
were offered. The bride gave her fox coat to one of the
secretaries saying, "I won't have any use for this where I
am going."

There is no record of what words were said by Hitler
to the woman he married on the day before he died, for the
next day, Hitler shot Eva Braun and then himself. Two
drums of oil had been ordered in preparation for their
death. The bodies of Hitler and Eva were then carried up
from the bunker to the outside, saturated with oil, and
cremated. When the Russians reached the bunker, they
found their charred bodies and, apparently, removed them.

Also in that bunker was Herr Goebbels, Hitler's minister
of propaganda, and Frau Goebbels and their six children.
Each child's name started with an "H" in honor of Hitler.
They had attended Hitler's wedding and, knowing that the
Russians were approaching, decided that they would also
commit suicide and that their six children must die with
them so that the Russians could not capture them.

Speer told me that he begged them not to kill the children; he offered to see that they would be cared for. He
entreated Frau Goebbels, who was in tears, to give the
children to him. Nevertheless, she submitted to Goebbels'
decision that the children were to die, also. A doctor used
a needle to inject poison in the children's arms. The eldest
resisted, screamed, and struggled to get away, knowing
what was happening. But she was held down by the doctor at Goebbels' orders. When the six children were

dead, Goebbels and his wife killed themselves. A drama of unbelievable horrors!

All of this which Speer described to me was confirmed by my friend, Arianne Shepherd, who is the half sister of Frau Goebbels. Arianne Shepherd is now an American citizen. She came to this country intrigued by the story of Dr. Sam Shepherd, a Clevelander, who was convicted of murdering his wife some ten years ago. The case rocked not only this country, but Europe.

I happened to be in Europe during the trial and even there it was the chief subject of conversation. Dr. Sam Shepherd was handsome, rich, and successful and his trial had the appeal of a great drama. It had the quality of a Greek tragedy; his mother committed suicide from grief and his father died soon afterward.

His conviction rested only on circumstantial evidence, for there were no witnesses to the murder. Arianne was convinced that he was innocent and that he had not had a fair trial. She came to Cleveland, sought out lawyers, paid for them herself, and ultimately Sam Shepherd was freed. The court held that he had not had a fair trial—that the newspapers had convicted him even before his case went to court. The case made legal history and Arianne was the one who fought for Dr. Shepherd's freedom. He was released, and they were married immediately. The next day they appeared on my show. The viewing audience watched with fascination, wondering what it was like to be married to a man who had been convicted of murder. During the interview he held on to Arianne's hand and was visibly nervous. What should have been one of the great love stories of the decade ended miserably with a divorce. It certainly was not Arianne's fault, she did everything to hold the marriage together. Ten years in jail must do things to a man's nervous system; perhaps he was no longer disciplined enough to take on the responsibility of marriage.

Why? What prompted a beautiful, cultured, well-bred young woman to take up the cause of a man convicted for murder remains enigmatic. I knew her through the years she fought this legal battle, years that must have been lonely and discouraging for her. I never understood why she gave so much to this man whom she had never met before she saw him behind bars, a convicted murderer.

So, there I sat in Speer's garden in Heidelberg, listening to him tell me of the last days of Frau Goebbels, the half-sister of Arianne, and the six children.

There in a garden with roses blooming, I thought, This is the eternal resurrection, life emerges from death. For how many generations will man remember this horrendous period of history, these years of the evil and horror of the Nazis, the sound of the trampling hordes of Nazi soldiers, the smell of burning flesh in the gas ovens?

It will become an evil dream—a nightmare that men lived through.

So I sat and listened to the story of Speer's twenty years in jail as an atonement for his allegiance to Hitler. The legacy of horror left to the world by the Nazis was the destruction of human values. And during the Olympics at Munich, where the Israelis were so brutally murdered, I remembered talking with Herr Speer, seeing him humbled and saddened.

Soon all the actors in this tragedy will be dead and I knew as I left the garden that I had heard part of the story of the travail of Germany which is already history. And as I said good-by to this courteous man, I recognized that the evil and the good in man were eternally contending for supremacy. Lured by the promises of Hitler, who was viciously evil, but who sang a song of war and victory to the German people which they embraced with fervor, Germany had become the citadel of evil.

No evil is completely destroyed nor are acts of goodness. It will take tremendous, unique acts of goodness on the part of the Germans to atone for the spiritual as well as physical wasteland of the Nazi days of supremacy.

I Threw Jerry Rubin
off My Show

This is a youth-oriented society, and the joke is on them because youth is a disease from which we all recover. How long does youth last? Ask the runner, the ballplayer, the football player, the heavyweight. At what time anatomically speaking does youth end? Is there a day, an hour, when the tender gift of youth is over? It represents only a small segment of our lives; but this whole generation's emphasis is on youth—the theater, music, clothes, language, everything geared to entertain and enshrine the first fourth of our lives. They have produced a life style contrary to elegance and beauty. *Hair* and *Jesus Christ Superstar*, as well as *Godspell*, are noisy, raucous, and vulgar. In *Hair* there is a loathsome copulating scene with a half dozen people performing the act at the same time The literature of youth is often full of orgasms and promiscuity. There was a time where the big moment in any novel occurred when the hero took the heroine in his arms and placed his lips on hers; then there were asterisks. Now there are no asterisks. The characters go directly to the bedroom where their sexual activities are described in detail. Youth has killed romance and their tasteless description of breasts as "boobs" is typical of their vulgarity.

They wear jeans, a legitimate article of apparel; but how dull, how uninteresting, a uniform worn by so many. In all of history there is no more colorless garb deliberately chosen. How can the art of coquetry be developed by a wearer of jeans? Long hair when it doesn't hide the face and shines with cleanliness can be quite beautiful, but the male hairdo and beard are another story. There is nothing the matter with a beard (if you like them) but in civilized society, grooming makes life a little easier. Unkempt, uncontrolled hair and beards are nauseating; and the Afro hairdo is a monstrosity whether in black or blond hair.

In my opinion this youth-oriented society has still to produce great architecture, music, poetry, or show a disciplined taste. It is sheer rubbish to write poetry or paint canvases that don't communicate. The writer and the painter may be having a glorious time creating, but creating means communicating, and I cannot take seriously some of the paintings and poetry I've looked at and read—the authors must be pulling my leg.

We worship youth. It is our national dream to preserve the illusion of youth, so women go on diets, equating youth with slenderness. The truth is if you are over thirty and your sex appeal depends on your weight, give it up, you haven't got any! The utter boredom of listening to talk about diets—doctors write books about their recommended diets and make oodles of money on the sale. Diet salons spring up, fashionable magazines carry diet lists. Everybody is doing it, it's the national theme song. Who is conditioning our men to desire flat-chested, hipless women? Women themselves are perpetrating the myth that to be thin is more desirable than to have a voluptuous figure. Who ever heard of a tree which looks like a sapling bearing fruit? But a woman who has had children must not betray it in her figure, for the American woman of the upper middle class and the wealthy have imposed thinness as the requisite of sex appeal.

Perhaps Rubens' women were a bit too buxom, but the incomparable Greek marbles, such as the Venus de Milo, never could have gotten into a size fourteen. Never mind if you are wise, or compassionate, or brilliant, or a wonderful friend and a great lover, or have lovely eyes; if you don't wear a size eight or ten, at the most, you are undesirable. Women impose this criteria and buyers in department stores and specialty shops buy for the skinny-small figure and effeminate males design the clothes. It's heresy to wear a size sixteen or even a fourteen; and, of course, the mature figure looks absurd in dresses made for tiny bodies. Yet it is the short skirt that prevails.

It is natural for women and men to want to look chic and smart, but this emphasis on weight is almost like a manifestation of national guilt that we have such an abundance of food while much of the world is starving. If I never see another chef salad, I shall weep no tears. Imagine the ridiculous state we have reached when Elizabeth Taylor is criticized because she isn't thin, and Jacqueline Onassis, with a figure that reminds one of a clothes tree, is the ideal sought by American women.

Youth is like an empty jug—the wine of life's experiences has not yet been matured. Give me a woman of forty or fifty and I'll tell you if she's beautiful by the lines of compassion around her eyes, the lines of laughter about her mouth, the proud way in which she carries her head, and the tender look in her eyes—that is a beautiful human being.

And yet in spite of this harsh criticism, the young are beautiful, long-legged with shiny eyes, with warm and generous instincts. They have no bitterness, laugh easily, love easily, and have a capacity to help when they are appealed to that is incredible. If only their life style were less undisciplined and noisy; if only their taste were as noble as their anti-war feelings, which they demonstrated again and again.

I threw Jerry Rubin off my program because his manners were bad and his arrogant attitude offensive. He wanted to show a picture of a nude with all the pubic hair showing.

"Why?" I said.

"Oh, ho," he cried triumphantly, "you don't approve of nudes."

"Why," I insisted, "do you want to show it? What is it germane to?"

No answer but another question hurled at me.

"Do you take pot?"

I looked astonished.

"No, of course not," he exclaimed before I had a chance to answer, "you drink and have a diseased liver."

Me, a diseased liver! I have the best functioning liver in the whole country!

Then he began a harangue on "the pigs," referring to the police. This was too much for me. I was suddenly filled with a violent rage. I stood up and shouted, "Get out, Mr. Rubin, get out!" And I snapped at the director, "Cut."

Mr. Rubin was astonished into silence. So was everyone else in the studio.

"You don't mean it," said a humbled Jerry Rubin.

I meant it. His manner, his attitude, his indictment of everything that was decent and disciplined made me sick. I was filled with wrath at the so-called hippie who disclaimed everything that the establishment stood for. Nudity, bare feet, the dirty coveralls, the unkempt hair; the whole defiance of grooming was their gift to our culture. If it was not for the establishment, who would take care of the sewers, water, electricity—everything needed for survival. Without the establishment that they scorned, they wouldn't have lasted a day.

So, "Get out, Mr. Rubin" was the culmination of watching these apes who endeavored to destroy a life style.

It happened that the former queen of Egypt, King Farouk's first wife, Fareda, was in the studio. She was scheduled to be interviewed immediately after Mr. Rubin. So after telling him to get out, I immediately called, "Now, Queen Fareda, please."

Having watched that scene, she was hesitant, not knowing what would happen to her. But she was charming, and by the time I started the interview I had recovered from the distaste of the interview with Rubin. I had no idea that the director kept the tape. I had presumed it would be wiped out. It was, on the contrary, used and created a storm of approval. Apparently, many of our viewers felt the same way. Wires, letters, flowers, candy, even wine poured in at least for a day.

I was Joan of Arc carrying the banner of revolt against the hippie. Of course, since then the hippie has been disappearing. They came like a plague, leaving dirt and filth and many a brokenhearted parent. But like all plagues, they burnt themselves out and now short hair, cleanliness, and good grooming are returning.

In the 1960s the 13,800,000 war babies between the ages of fourteen to twenty-four covered the land. There were more teen-agers in the sixties than at any other time in our history. They silenced their parents and developed their own inelegant life style. In the seventies the number of teen-agers will decline significantly and the young will no longer be dominant.

At another time I refused to appear on the six-thirty news show where I do a commentary each evening. One of the radio stations did a show with everyone in the nude. One of our photographers wanted to film it. He was told he would be allowed to film it only if he, too, would be clothesless. He removed his clothes and filmed the program.

When I came into the newsroom, I was told the film was going to be used. I asked why.

"It's a good story."

My reaction was that it was fit for one thing—to be flushed down the toilet.

"If you use it," I said, "I will not appear on the show."

There was dead silence in the newsroom—no one supported me. So, I went in to see Mr. Perris, the station manager, a man of extraordinary perception and great intellect, who was sitting calmly at his desk. "What's up?" he asked.

"I'm not appearing on the show tonight."

"Why, are you ill? What's the matter?"

"No, I'm not physically ill but I'm mentally nauseated. I'm sick of having my life style besmirched and I propose expressing my disdain and disapproval. And if they use that film on the news, I will not appear."

They used the story and showed the nudes, and Mr. Perris suggested that I write a statement as to why I wouldn't appear. Since I don't type (I write my editorials longhand) the manager typed it out. He may have thought it was a good story, but he obviously thought my objection to it was also a good story.

The anchorman read my statement as to why I didn't appear. They were, undoubtedly, right. The nude show was a flamboyant news story. On the other hand, in news, with the enormous impact TV has, it's up to those who appear to maintain a standard of good taste, good manners, good English, and integrity. I do not believe that the standards must be low, that one's vocabulary must be simple. To the contrary, people have much more sense, much more appreciation of the good and the fine and the important than they are credited with and it's up to TV performers, writers, and producers to recognize that fact.

By what right do they presume to offer the lowest, the most beastly aspects of man. Why should the vocabulary be geared to fifth grade level. This is a mighty nation, the mightiest and the richest, with an incomparable heritage, a nation of liberty and courage. Why should we deny high standards of conduct and taste? If the movies influenced our life style, TV can be more powerful. Is it so desirable to present the perverts, the vulgar, the law breakers? What's so wrong about showing the good and the noble?

When Mr. Burt Reynolds' nude picture appeared in *Cosmopolitan* magazine, with his hands coyly hiding his sex organs, he caused a greater sensation than a nude photograph of the late Marilyn Monroe would have created, and why not? If *Playboy* had grown fat and rich in displaying the female body, why shouldn't Mr. Reynolds make some money? Was the picture pornographic? Is *Playboy* with its nude center female strip pornographic? Are the waitresses without tops part of pornography? Great paintings of nude figures by Goya, Picasso, Michelangelo—who when he was criticized for his nude Herculean figures on the Sistine Chapel pointed out that when God created man, he was not clothed—are not pornography.

The difference is the motive. One is for beauty's sake, the other to titillate the sex appetite. The objection is that humans are not animals who copulate anywhere. To strip passion of beauty, of wooing, of tenderness, is ugly. Discipline is necessary to achieve good taste, good manners, good grooming, and control of all our passions, not only sex. Without discipline only vulgarity and brutality are left.

We live in a clothes-oriented society and the nudes are the exhibitionists. They are the odd ones—those who believe that taking off their clothes will lead them to fame and fortune. If this is the path Mr. Reynolds chooses to walk, to decorate *Cosmopolitan* magazine, they deserve each other.

Kent

In Kent at the "U" on the fourth of May 1970, the day dawned like any other May day. The dandelions were in full bloom, covering the green, unkempt lawns. Lilacs were heavy with dew and perfume. On that day the students and faculty rose and prepared as on any other day to go to classes. In the dormitories voices were heard intermingled with laughter. Cooks were preparing the coffee and eggs. Girls were brushing their hair, watching their reflections in the mirrors. Boys were leaving their shirts hanging over their blue jeans or trousers, some whistling with the joy of living, others worried about classroom assignments that were not completed. Radios were blasting, the hustle and bustle sounds of the beginning of the day's activity pervaded the air.

The driver of a truck on his way to Cleveland slowed up as he passed the campus and noted that the students were not about as yet. The day, he thought, will be beautiful and in a short while the campus will be swarming with students. He was unaware, as was everyone else, that a skeleton rider on a skeleton horse was galloping toward the campus with the banner of death unfurled. Before the sun was midway in the afternoon sky four students would be lying dead on the grass and nine wounded. The stain on the honor of Ohio that day was indelibly woven into the history of the state.

What had the students done? What was their crime that they were so wantonly, so unnecessarily, so pointlessly shot down to die? They had committed no crime, had uttered no threats, many of them just happened to be in the milling crowd walking across campus. The crowd had gathered on the campus for a protest meeting against the war. Did the National Guard receive some official order, or did they become nervous and shoot randomly? For suddenly a volley of shots rang out across the campus and the beauty of the day was marred by this senseless act of the killing of those who committed no crime or act of violence. No single excuse has been found for this killing. Even an accused murderer or robber or kidnaper has a chance in the courts to disclaim any guilt and a jury of his peers will listen to his defense. But what chance did these dead students have? Did anyone accuse them of a crime? Were they told why they died? It was a senseless killing, as senseless as a tornado which tears down a tree just because it happens to be in the path of the storm.

There were no guns in the hands of the four who were killed and the nine who were wounded—they had no weapons, no iron rods in their hands, they were giving no speeches. Their sin was protesting against the war and the four that were killed were only bystanders. They were there to see what was going on; they were students who were curious about the excitement. There were crowds gathering on the campus to protest the war so they came along to see what was happening. No one told them that the governor of the state had called out the National

Guard. The governor apparently decided it would show these long-haired troublemakers that protest meetings were not to be tolerated. There was some jostling, shouting and rock throwing but what prompted the National Guard to shoot? And who gave the National Guard the bullets? Who ordered the use of them? Since when do we shoot our own children? Ask the parents of these young people how they feel. When will their anguish be over? Tortured at the thought that their children were killed and without a reason, they exist with a pain in their hearts.

So they died and I came back to Cleveland and went on the air and showed my emotion and anger about the killings. As I recounted their deaths I called it murder, for these four were no housebreakers, they were no killers, no drug addicts, no muggers, no rapists.

The reaction to my report was unbelievable. The switchboard lit up like the proverbial Christmas tree and for the remainder of the night the calls came in excoriating me! "Why," they demanded, "are you sorry for those deaths? Too bad the National Guard didn't kill more. Those good-for-nothing bums, smart alecks—that's what they are. It's about time someone put them in their place. Good for the National Guard."

I was appalled at their resentment against the rebellion of the young who refused to believe that the war in Vietnam was necessary for our safety. Unfortunately the nobility of their convictions was belittled because their hair was long, and they wore beards and blue jeans.

Literally thousands of letters poured into the station, most of them condemning me for my emotional reaction. Did they want me to remain stolid and report the deaths as though I were talking about how to make applesauce or some such pedestrian subject? They resented my tears as well as the students' rally protesting the war. Suddenly it was the students on one side and the establishment on the other and the students were fair game. Why did Governor Rhodes take no action? What did the then attorney general of the United States, Mr. Mitchell, mean when he ordered "no investigation"? Why was the National Guard sent to Kent with real bullets in their guns? Why were many who wrote to me satisfied with the killings? Why was the hatred so great against the murdered students? So violent was the outcry against me because I had wept that I offered to resign, and that superb, highly perceptive manager of the television station where I have worked for over a quarter of a century and to whom I offered my resignation, said, "Nonsense, you are nine feet tall." I took so many calls—ninety-five per cent against the students—that I became jittery and stopped taking calls, but the letters came pouring in and I groaned as bag after bag was delivered.

There were many individuals who were as outraged as I was, but the majority were against the students. One lovely thing did happen; outside my door the next morning, I found a basket of spring flowers and card which read, "We wept with you last night," signed, "Some students."

When I interviewed Albert Speer, I told him that the most terrible legacy of the Nazis was the destruction of human values. So it has come to pass—the murder of these young students, the horror in Munich at the Olympics, the hijacking of planes, and now Watergate. We have no great leaders today who have a shining vision of a good and moral world. We are too sophisticated to be good, that is too simplistic. If we are evil, we must be psychoanalyzed. We have lost the path leading to righteousness.

I went back to Kent on a sunlit day in May and walked over the campus where the tragedy occurred. For the four who were killed there will be no sunshine. They sleep their eternal sleep lighted only by the stars and the moon. What had they done, what crime that they should meet death? Their eyes were innocent; their hands bore no weapons; their hearts were pure with the hope of peace in Vietnam; and for this hope they died, indiscriminately shot by the National Guard. I call your names: Allison Krause, William Schroeder, Jeffrey Miller, and Linda Scheuer, so that we remember that on this day the blood of the very young, not much older than children, stained the earth of our land because they dreamed, these young, of a world without war.

Man's Destiny

I watched a remarkable television show one night—a pictorial report of salmon swimming upstream, obeying the pattern of their destiny implanted in their genes and chromosomes. Wildly, madly, unswervingly, they tumble over the rapids on their way to obey the very reason for their existence, to mate and then to die. There is no escape for them. This is the ritual of their lives circumscribed by their heritage, implanted in their bodies through millenniums of time. Who can calculate, who can describe the overpowering urge that sends them on to the hour of their fulfillment and then to die. Perhaps there is an ecstasy in those hours and a rapture that makes death a small price to pay.

But I am not a salmon. No sexual ecstasy would be enough to accept death. Most of us are willing to suffer the anguish of a lost love rather than face death; The Romeos and Juliets are deviates. Then, what is this quiet but overpowering sense of exultation and resignation I perceive as I enter what must surely be the last decade of my life. Is it that I expect a form of immortality? I must say "no" to that.

I recall my mother one October day, as she approached

ninety, sitting at the window in her room and looking out
on the garden. There were a few roses still blooming.
"Soon," she said, "these roses will be gone, withered and
swept away by the wind, their beauty and perfume forgotten, and soon it will be with me."

But if I am not like the salmon, neither am I like the
rose. For as I contemplate the long, long journey of creation across aeons of time, starting from the one cell to this
final moment when man is about to go on his journey to
the stars, I am filled with a pride and even a joy. I, like
millions, have carried the genes that ultimately produced
what for lack of a better word we call the soul. From a
thousand thousand generations there emerged this wonderful, miraculous thing called the mind and from it a
certain nobility, a certain capacity for feeling, an occasional
glimpse of an individual endowed with goodness and an
ability to understand and feel another person's pain and
grief. When was the first time man transferred his concern
for his child to other human beings? When did human beings develop the capacity for pity, for compassion, for the
heroic moment of sacrificing one's self for another? Men
enter burning buildings to rescue others, they crawl under
fire in battle to aid a wounded comrade. They climb moun-
tains to rescue stranded climbers. They share their food.
The most passionate example was that of Jesus. Believer
and non-believer in His divinity must yet recognize that
the supreme moment of His death became sanctified because His crucifixion was to ensure those who believed entrance to eternal life.

That it may only be a legend does not invalidate its
significance. If men endowed Jesus' death with supreme
sublimity, a death accepted by Jesus to redeem men's souls,
to dwell forever in God's arms, it dramatizes the emergence of a new concept that proclaims sacrifice of one's
self for another. It may be that through the ages the con-

cept of sacrifice for another human being was corrupted and bent to evil but the new dimension of giving of one's self for another had been proclaimed and emerges constantly, crowning man with a nobility.

Here on a hospital table in an operating room lies a man soon to surrender to the removal of one of his kidneys so that another man may live. In that act of sacrifice he affirms the evolution of man. As the surgeon's knife cuts deeply into the flesh, the act itself becomes an affirmation of the new role of man in evolution. Here in this brilliantly lit operating room are doctors and nurses attending this extraordinary act of bravery, transcending the heretofore overwhelming impulse for the safety of one's self, a gamble with death itself. In the long, long journey of man's evolution, this is a superb moment of defiance of the powerful instinct of self-preservation.

It reveals the growing capacity for man to surrender his own life for another. This is an emergence of a quality that transcends the survival equipment with which nature endowed all living creatures. Is it possible that we have taken nature and remolded it nearer to "our hearts' desire" or was it always there waiting to take over the overpowering instinct for survival.

The supreme renunciation of one's own life to save another's life is an almost incredible act on the part of a human being whose instinct for survival is rooted so deeply in his being.

This need torments man—the need to justify his humanness, which differentiates him from the lower forms through which he was evolved. Who placed this need, this hunger for nobility on the brow of man? Where in the dark ascending stairway of evolution did this selfless light appear, engulfing and clothing the soul of man with radiance?

Some small part of that radiance is mine also, for in

that long pilgrimage, I too have taken part. Some small act of surrendering self to another's need. Who can say where this pilgrimage will take us?

There are those who were vociferous in their complaints about our trips to the moon. "Why spend the money," they cried, "on such a wild adventure? What good will it do us?" No one knows. But the urge to make the pilgrimage into space is overpowering. It is built into our being even as the salmon answers the laws of their existence. Somewhere in space must be our destiny. Somewhere in space we may meet creation itself. The beginnings of all things mature and grow only to crumble into dust; but for man there is a powerful revulsion at the thought of annihilation; that very revulsion validates the hope of some continuation after death. The salmon does not suffer from the knowledge that death awaits him, but in man there is a maddening need to believe that whatever the pattern, there must be a logic, a purpose, a plan.

To reach the stars our pace has been so slow that the progress, unless viewed from centuries, is almost indiscernible. But today we stand on tiptoe to catch the secrets of the stars. Does anyone really believe that the need to go into space will be stopped by a budget or a brutal cynicism?

From somewhere in the vastness of space so infinite that a finite mind recoils from it, there was a beginning and to that beginning, which must be creation itself, we may return when we journey to the stars.

If man bought existence with mortality as a down payment, somewhere in space we may cancel that mortgage and learn what the secret of life and creation really is.

"Who am I?" will be the question hurled at creation and, "What is my destiny?" Perhaps then we shall have the answer to, "What is life and why do I die?"

Mrs. O'Grady

How many silent, uneventful tragedies are played out in thousands of marriages? How many women stay married though they experience a dull, nagging unhappiness; stay because after years of marriage they have developed no skill to qualify for a job and if they are over forty, their age is an additional hindrance. If ever there are lives led in "quiet desperation," they are marriages without friendliness, dignity, love, and passion. Mrs. O'Grady's marriage exemplified this dull, unhappy condition. But the morning I watched Mrs. O'Grady walking down the street observing the peonies, which were in full bloom, she was a happy woman.

It was early in June and only preschool children were on the street with their bicycles and kiddy cars. The milkman came out of one of the houses.

"Good morning, Mrs. O'Grady."

And from the rooms behind the screen door Mrs. O'Malley, a neighbor, was heard to say, "You can fix your clock by Mrs. O'Grady. It's always ten minutes to twelve when she walks past this house."

Mrs. O'Grady nodded to the milkman and continued on her way. At the corner she was stopped by Mrs. O'Malley's mother, who was returning home loaded with tomatoes and onions for a soup she planned to make that evening.

"How are you, Mrs. O'Grady? It's such a beautiful day. Are you out shopping?"

"No, I'm on my way to the Roman Gardens for lunch."

"It's funny," said Mrs. O'Malley's mother when she reached her daughter's house, "every Wednesday and Saturday Mrs. O'Grady goes to the Roman Gardens and always at the same time. She leaves her house at eleven-thirty because she always passes our house at exactly ten of twelve. She never did that while her husband was alive. I wonder what's come over her?"

But Mrs. O'Grady, unaware of the conversation about her habits, continued on her way. She loved the walk, the streets, and the trees, and the sound of voices and children laughing and yelling to each other. She counted the geraniums in one of the yards. She stopped to watch the painters bringing life and whiteness to a house. Trucks went by and automobiles. All of these things were a sign of life and Mrs. O'Grady was glad she was alive and free. "Free," she said to herself. Now she was on her way to the Gardens and soon she would be seated at a table under an awning ordering her lunch.

Mrs. O'Grady continued down the street, turned the corner, and came to the fenced-in garden with tables and awnings attached to the Roman Gardens. If Mrs. O'Grady had reflected on the name of the restaurant she might have wondered what resemblance this small but cheerful restaurant had to the grandeur that once was Rome's. In the winter, the diners used the inside dining room, which was decorated with American and Italian flags and a mural of

Venice. The restaurant was patronized by some of the faculty of the school near by and an office building three or four blocks away.

Mrs. O'Grady felt great pride in ordering her lunch and leaving a small tip. She was still drunk with her freedom. She could go out for lunch when she wanted to and where. For ten sweet months she had been free. Mr. O'Grady died after twenty-five years of marriage. For almost that length of time she had been only a shadow of Mr. O'Grady's. She had to get up before Mr. O'Grady so that his breakfast was ready. Mr. O'Grady would eat only homemade bread. He refused to eat a cookie unless she baked it. No jam, no pickles, no noodles unless she made them. He wore a clean shirt every day and he hated shirts done by a laundry and he didn't trust the "Chinks" he told Mrs. O'Grady. So Mrs. O'Grady had to launder his shirts. He came home for lunch so she never could get away. He refused to go out in the evenings to the movies. Why should he bother to go out when TV was there and besides it was cheaper.

"Pay two-and-a-half dollars for a movie, not me!" he stormed.

Mrs. O'Grady wanted a new dress to go to church. How many dresses, by the Holy Virgin, did she need to cover herself! There was never an argument. Mr. O'Grady never argued, he just decided. When the neighbors invited them over for a glass of beer, Mr. O'Grady said, "No, I don't want to associate with those people and I don't want to invite them here." Mrs. O'Grady wanted to plant some tulips in their back yard. Why tulips! Plant something that we can eat—tomatoes, celery. Slowly Mrs. O'Grady began to hate her husband. She had been a happy buxom girl when he married her and she was quite prepared to be fond of him even if there was no great love affair. But she never forgot her wedding night—his clumsiness and his brutal possession of her. What was worse, he made a ritual of it. Always on Saturday night he would make his position as husband clearly understood. No tenderness, no love-making—a Saturday night possession just as regularly as he ate his dinner. Mrs. O'Grady grew to dislike him, then she hated him, and then she feared him. Every penny that she spent had to be accounted for. She hated washing his clothes, she hated hearing him brush his teeth, she loathed his burping at the table, his vulgar expelling of gas.

There came a Saturday night when Mrs. O'Grady refused to go to bed. "I'm not coming to bed. I'm going to watch TV."

Mr. O'Grady was nonplussed. This had never happened before. Well, he wasn't going to beg her. Hell, she wasn't much of a lay—like a log. She was no pleasure.

So, Mr. O'Grady went to sleep, but on Monday when he left for work instead of the three dollars he left every day for food there was only two-fifty. Mrs. O'Grady said not a word but bought less food. The next Saturday Mr. O'Grady retired and called, "Are you coming to bed?"

Mrs. O'Grady answered, "No, I'm going to watch TV."

Mr. O'Grady made no response but on Monday he left only two dollars and did not come home for lunch. The next Saturday she refused again and on Monday Mr. O'Grady left only a dollar and a half. The following Saturday his voice came from the bedroom, "Well, are you coming?" This time she didn't even answer him.

Mr. O'Grady said nothing but as the days went on, the dollar which he left every day was hardly enough for the one evening meal. With the price of food it was impossible to provide a full meal and now she had nothing to eat during the day except a meager breakfast and an inadequate evening meal. She was sure that Mr. O'Grady had his meal before he came home. The next Saturday when her husband demanded to know if she was coming to bed, she came. She was hungry and she hated him but her hunger was greater than her hate.

So on Monday, the usual three dollars were put on the table for food that day. She ate ravenously and bought meat and candy and cake. She couldn't get enough. She ate and ate and as the weeks went on she continued to gorge. She put on weight. She became heavy. None of her clothes fit her. She was obsessed with the idea of food. She thought of it all the time. Saturday nights were the price she paid for food. While her husband possessed her, uttering his unpoetical grunts and groans, she dreamed of a seven-layer cake, of banana splits with nuts and chocolate sauce and whipped cream. She could see in her mind a table with a great ham and candied brown crust, a turkey stuffed with rice stuffing. She could smell the roast beef and taste the mashed potatoes. The longer his possession of her lasted, the more food she imagined.

Now the three dollars wasn't enough. She informed her husband that the cost of food had gone up. So he added fifty cents to the three dollars.

The next Saturday night when he called she said, "Not unless you give me another dollar for my food allowance."

"Go to hell," he answered. "I don't need you."

On Monday he reduced the amount he left for her to buy food. But all week he kept thinking about her and the more he thought about Saturday night the more his desire for her grew. So, he agreed to give her the additional amount.

"But this is it; no more money."

"Then," she retorted, "there will be no Saturday nights for you." It is strange, she thought, but I know I'm winning and he knows that I am. Possessing her on Saturday had become an obsession with him.

Unwilling to admit to her that the Saturday night in bed with her was important to him, he added the half dollar. Also, he found himself enjoying her more as she gained weight so that when she asked for more money for food, he doled out the additional dollars.

Her clothes were too tight for her. She was able to buy only one dress and this she used when she went shopping and to church. She no longer cared whether he gave her money to buy clothes. Her only interest was in food and the highlight of the day was the trip to the grocery store. Mr. Angelo, the grocery man, said to his wife, "The O'Gradys must have someone living with them. They spend so much more money for food than they ever did."

Mrs. O'Grady had been in the habit of saving a certain amount of food every week and then bringing it to the church for distribution to some of the needy families to supplement their welfare checks. Even Mr. O'Grady did not object to this. The church was the church and Father Miletti had made it clear that O'Grady had a good job and a good income, that he was a Catholic and charity was necessary to be a good Catholic.

Father Miletti observed that Mrs. O'Grady had not dropped her basket off at the parish house as usual. When a month went by without Mrs. O'Grady appearing, he decided to stop and inquire if she was well. Mrs. O'Grady heard his car stop in front of the house. She saw him come up the walk and hid so that she would not have to answer the doorbell. She had no intention of sharing her food. She was too hungry and too fearful that she would not have enough. She had heard that if you eat more than usual your stomach stretches and you need more food. She didn't care; what else was there in life? He never took her out. He wouldn't give her money to belong to a club. She couldn't play canasta as other women did. Mr. O'Grady said no money for such foolishness. Once when she had nagged him he came over and slapped her. She should have left him but where would she go? She had no family. Her parents were long since dead. She had uncles and aunts in Italy but how would she ever get there? With what money? She loathed the Saturday nights in bed with him. Perhaps it wouldn't have been so distasteful if it had not had the regulatory aspect—if occasionally he had desired her on a Tuesday or a Thursday. But now she realized he could beat her into submission by leaving her just enough money for food to keep from starving. But her revenge was to make him pay for the Saturday nights with more money, which in turn brought her more food.

Her hate for him was now part of her being, like the air she breathed. It enveloped her and the only time she was free of it was when she was sleeping or eating. She forgot there was a time when she had not hated him, at least accepted and endured him without much feeling.

One Saturday night he went to bed earlier than usual but did not call her. Perhaps he had fallen asleep, but if she did not come to him he would punish her by leaving her no money. So, indifferent to anything but the surety of food, for the first time in all their married life she voluntarily went to their bed. Mr. O'Grady made no sound, nor did he stir as she got into bed. Her weight made the bed creak and groan. Could he be that sound asleep or had he decided not to use her anymore for this sex titillation. She was panicky. What would she do if he no longer wanted her? She moved close to him and suddenly fear struck her. He felt cold. She sat upright and shook him. She called to him. She got out of bed and took his arms. They fell from her hands lifeless. Filled with terror, she ran to her neighbors. The doctor came, but Mr. O'Grady was dead at fifty-four years of age from, the doctor said, a massive heart attack.

Mrs. O'Grady found that her parsimonious husband, who had been so stingy and denied her everything, had saved his money and to her astonishment he was worth a hundred thousand dollars. She was a rich widow, she was free of the Saturday night ritual, and she no longer dreamed of food. It was there for her taking, all that she wanted.

Now she had a half-dozen dresses and the basket of food went to the parish house every week. Father Miletti preached a sermon describing the beautiful life of the O'Gradys and how brave Mrs. O'Grady was in covering up her grief and loneliness. The neighbors said she was losing weight because of her grief.

That was over a year ago. Now Mrs. O'Grady sat at the table under an umbrella ordering her food. Every Wednesday and Saturday the waitress expected her. "And how are you today? Mrs. O'Grady, the soup today is minestrone and it's good."

She watched the light and shadows play over the table. She listened to the chatter of the patrons at the other tables. How pleasant it was to sit here every Wednesday and Saturday noon. The Saturday noon was a celebration —freedom from the Saturday night ritual when her husband was alive.

Her food came. First the soup, then a meat and vegetable course, and always a dessert.

Her waitress as she cleared the table for the dessert said, "My, Mrs. O'Grady, you just nibble at your food. You leave enough on your plate to feed another person."

Mrs. O'Grady smiled and if Mrs. O'Grady could be described as radiant at any time her smile would have been a radiant one. She assumed an aristocratic smile as becomes a lady and answered, "I've always been a light eater. My late husband used to comment on it."

"Boy," said the waitress, "it must be wonderful to have had such a husband for all these years you were married and then to have him provide so well for you. You know, Mrs. O'Grady, not many widows can afford to dine here as often as you do and not even eat all the food."

"Yes," said Mrs. O'Grady, "it is nice. I don't have to eat all the food as there is always another day."

As Mrs. O'Grady left, the waitress picked up her tip and thought to herself, Why can't I find a husband who would take such good care of me?

Lilacs

One night I was having dinner with my friend Lacy, her husband Paul, and their twin girls. The girls were teasing their mother because of her voice, which has a slight "Come up and see me some time" tone.

"Sexy," the girls said, "that's what you are, Mom, sexy. Hey, Dad, is Mom sexy?"

"My wife Lacy," he said, "is a fraud. Sexy? Not by a long shot. She is as cold as the proverbial iceberg and not the least bit interested in men."

"Lacy," he told me as he filled my wineglass, "is a wonderful wife. She keeps my house running smoothly, there isn't a wrinkle in it, she fusses over the children till they are spoiled beyond reason; why her linen closets keep her awake worrying for fear every towel isn't in place; she has a nervous spasm if the silver isn't put away in exact order; if she knows that a butter knife is in the wrong section, she won't go to bed until it's fixed properly. And she would rather go to bed and read than go out with me. The only men she really likes are the ones she finds in books."

Sometimes his daughters would tease him and say, "But, Dad, how come mother married you? You are no story-book hero, though we must admit that she could have done much worse."

"That, my children," he answered, "is one of the seven wonders of the modern world."

At which point Lacy interrupted with, "What are the other wonders, dear?"

"Well, one of the other wonders certainly is the fact that you have lived with me for twenty-two years," answered her husband.

"Poor mother," said Lacy's eighteen-year-old twins in a patronizing manner. "Mother reads her books and hardly knows the facts of life. Mother, darling, did you ever have a flirtation with anyone but Dad?"

"Your mother is too intellectual, she reads too much, men leave her strictly alone so I never have any trouble. Besides, your mother wouldn't know what to do with the attentions of any man but myself, my dears," spoke up Lacy's husband.

To which Lacy might have responded, "And of which I receive very little."

I was amused. How typically male and husbandlike, I thought, because just before dinner Lacy had told me about an episode that occurred a week before. She explained that her husband Paul was a fine chap but pre-occupied with his business, his golf, and his dancing. For the most part he took her for granted and forgot to tell her he loved her. After all, they had been married for twenty-two years. Lacy was eighteen when he wooed her, and a man couldn't keep on being ardent and acting silly after so many years. Besides, Lacy liked to read, he liked to dance. Lacy didn't. She wasn't a good dancer to begin with, she had little talent for it. Paul, on the other hand, adored it and was forever looking for a new partner. He would regale Lacy with his new partner's dancing ability, her gusto, her high spirits, and her looks.

Long ago Lacy had stopped being hurt at his interest in his dancing partners; she learned that they meant nothing in Paul's life. But he had so much physical energy, he was so vain of his dancing skill, that he was not happy unless he was active; and he was completely unconscious of the effect on Lacy.

Of course, what Paul never knew, because Lacy never revealed it, was her hurt pride that she was not adequate and that Paul needed other interests to keep him happy. So, Lacy found refuge in books while Paul went dancing.

Lacy could never sit still if anything in the house needed attention. A chair that had a soiled spot—she had to clean it; if a shirt was minus a button, Lacy had to sew it on immediately; if the linen closet was slightly disarranged, Lacy had to fix it; if a letter of condolence had to be written, Lacy did it that day not the next. Paul said she liked doing those things; they were her life, she wouldn't be happy without them. But the fact was that Lacy was forever doing the things she didn't want to do. It seemed to her every morning when she rose that a mountain was piled up in front of her and absurdly every day, the same routine, unpiling the small tasks that made that mountain. She fretted inwardly at the passing of the days bound by such details, but unless the house was in complete order and the family routine taken care of, she was uncomfortable.

This particular evening, she told me, she was restless. She began to wonder what was the matter with her anyway, that these hours away from everyone were the only ones she enjoyed. Even when her husband came in and she heard his one hundred and eighty pounds sink into the other bed, it was infringement on her privacy. There was a subtle change even in the pleasure of her reading when he came to bed. The fact that Paul was a fine man and a decent human being had nothing to do with her hunger for privacy, but she had never had the courage to tell him that she wanted a room of her own where no one could enter.

Oh well, she had thought of this for so long that there was no need for dwelling on it; apparently she didn't want the room more than she was willing to hurt Paul's feelings. She glanced over to her desk. It was her birthday and some presents were piled on it. There was the fifty-dollar check from her husband. "You buy what you want, Lacy, I don't know how to buy the fancy things you like."

Her two daughters were at a house party. They had phoned that they would buy her present when they returned. For a moment Lacy thought to herself, "Why didn't they plan it before they left?" But she dismissed the idea as an unreasonable one.

But if Lacy had known it, that was exactly what everyone said about her—Lacy is so reasonable, and because she was, her family was forever taking advantage of her. She was constantly doing things for them, making life easier and smoother. Was Paul bored and did he want to dance? Lacy, though she hated dancing, would get up a party. If the girls wanted a luncheon, it was Lacy who arranged it, because they said, "She does it so effortlessly and it's always a success if Mother arranges it." Lacy knew that she was exploited but then she loved them, and, anyway, what else was there in life? But sometimes, just as tonight, she wished that she wasn't forever creating a situation for someone else to play the lead. She would like to have someone arrange something for her so that she could be the center of attention.

There was another present on the desk, a white silk smock with green trimmings. This was from Alice, Lacy's oldest friend. Alice Gruvnor and Lacy had been friends since childhood. Lacy remembered Alice as a fat jolly girl, and very rich. She always wore wonderful hats; one in particular was decorated with three plumes. Alice's father served champagne at dinner and had some wonderful horses. Alice was gay and had dates in spite of her lack of looks. Her father was too rich, the wise ones said, for Alice to be obliged to stay home; she will always have dates and someone will marry her for her father's assets. But Lacy recalled that was not what happened at all.

Alice's father lost his money and a young man, who was to become her husband, fell in love with her. It started with his feeling sorry for her, which is not too unsuccessful a premise for falling in love, if it can be established. Alice had a theory that if you could create a situation where the man you wanted saw you in tears, the battle was half won. Lacy used to poo-poo Alice's ideas, but Alice remained firm.

"You just start crying when you are with a male that isn't interested in you and see what happens," she insisted.

Lacy never was sure how much of anything Alice said she really believed or how much was pure stubbornness; having made a statement nothing could make her change.

Alice worried about Lacy and her habits. "For goodness sake, Lacy," she would say, "don't be such an old poke in the mud, forever going to bed with your old books."

To which Paul, if he were present, would invariably rejoin, "Oh, let her be, Alice. After all, my wife goes to bed with distinguished men. I bet she's probably been to bed with more men than any other woman of her generation. Last week it was Alexander the Great, this week it's Henry of Navarre."

Lacy picked up her book again but images kept coming back to her of Alice's father, a handsome, debonair man who had been very fond of Lacy. He used to say to her, "Lacy, when spring comes a slight madness takes possession of men. I always go fishing to keep out of danger. Watch out, Lacy dear, for the spring days when the lilacs are in bloom."

Lacy reflected that she never saw a lilac tree in bloom without remembering Mr. Gruvnor's admonition about madness in spring taking possession of men. Well, it was springtime now and the lilac bushes were heavy with purple and white blossoms. Suddenly Lacy got out of bed and slipped into her mules. There was a lilac tree in her neighbor's yard. She knew they were gone for the weekend and she decided she would do what she had always wanted to do, bury her head and shoulders in a lilac tree heavy with blossoms and rain.

She knew if any of the family should see her they would say, "One of Mother's funny notions." But Lacy had a passion for beautiful and poetic sensations and perhaps old Mr. Gruvnor had been right, in spring there is a slight madness that takes possession of men's souls. But none of the family was home so she could indulge in her moon-light madness uncriticized. She put a long raincoat over her robe and walked over to her neighbor's garden. The sky was still dark but the rain had stopped. Everything she touched was wet, but the lilacs were sweet and per-fumed. She kept her face in the blossoms and the rain-drops on the flowers covered her face and throat with a perfumed coolness. Lacy tore off a branch and walked over to the terrace where there were some benches under an awning; her raincoat prevented her from getting too wet. What a night of loveliness full of perfume and flowers all magically cooled with rain. What a time for madness, Lacy thought.

The quiet of the night was broken by the swishing of footsteps over the gravel path. She immediately identified the intruder; it was Tom Blake, their neighbor across the way. He stopped, thoroughly startled.

"For goodness sake, Lacy, what are you doing here?"

"It's spring madness, Tom," answered Lacy.

"What? Lacy, you sound fantastic," replied Tom. "Now, I'm out deliberately to do a fancy piece of robbing. Didn't you know I was quite a thug? I knew the Valentines were out of town and so while they are gone I thought I'd do a bit of thieving and take some of their lilacs. But you, Lacy, what are you doing here sitting on that bench looking like a wooded nymph in your white robe and green raincoat?"

But without giving her a chance to answer, he continued, "The truth is I'm inordinately fond of lilacs. I've been trying to get a tree planted in our garden, but you know Ruth, my wife, doesn't care for them, she says they're too old-fashioned. So if I can't have one in my own yard there is just nothing left to do but let the Valentines furnish me with their lilacs. I warned them I'd be rifling their garden this spring. You know, Lacy, lilacs always make me a little dizzy, they remind me too much of my very young days and my early loves."

Once again, Lacy remembered Mr. Gruvnor's injunction, "Careful of the springtime, men always grow a little mad then." How long ago was it that she heard Alice's father say that, a thousand years ago or only yesterday?

Was she a little mad too to come out into the moonless night in the rain to smell lilacs? She knew perfectly well that her husband and her girls would think she was silly and with a patronizing but affectionate tone they would say, "Mother is a little heady with poetry but she's a darling."

"Am I little queer?" thought Lacy. "My friends don't go wandering around in gardens at midnight smelling lilacs; my friends don't insist on being perfumed and bedolled in chiffon negligées after a day of mundane duties to read pondersome books. What is the matter with me?" And now here she was caught in someone else's garden in a negligée and raincoat and mules, madly sniffing lilacs. Tom must think she was crazy. She certainly hoped he wouldn't go around telling their friends of her midnight meanderings.

But Tom, in a matter-of-fact voice said, "Here, Lacy, take that raincoat off and give me some of it to sit on; this bench is so wet."

But a stir of the trees brought some raindrops on Lacy's robe and Tom put his arm around her to protect her from the wet. Lacy shivered.

Tom looked down at her. "Cold, Lacy? You know you are a damn good-looking woman and it's lucky for you that I'm just plain Tom Blake, an honorable guy with perfectly decent intentions toward my neighbor, or I would start making love to you right now."

Lacy smiled. "Tom, are you slightly mad too?"

"No, Lacy, I'm not. I wish I were, because you are not only good to look at, but you are soft and you smell better than the lilacs. But I'm a prudent insurance executive and I have two boys at school who I earnestly hope will someday marry your daughters, so I can have you in the family. But I'm not mad; so you see, you have nothing to fear from me. But sit here awhile with me. If they notice your absence or mine they will never come hunting in a wet garden looking for us."

But he held Lacy's hand firmly and then suddenly he leaned toward her and kissed her.

"Tom, let me go," said Lacy, as women have said for a thousand years.

But Tom gently pushed her face back until her hair touched the wet purple blossoms. "Now, Lacy, here with the lilac blossoms circling your face, I shall kiss you, and every spring forever I will remember that once a lilac tree bore a nymph whom I kissed."

So Lacy closed her eyes and Tom's lips touched hers and the smell of rain and the wet leaves and the heavy lilac perfume and the moonless night surrounded and filled her consciousness. Then Tom let her go and Lacy walked swiftly back into the house.

The next day a box was delivered to Lacy containing her green raincoat and on top of the coat was a cluster of lilac blossoms. Fortunately, when she opened the box, no one of the family was around to ask questions concerning her raincoat and why it arrived in a box with lilacs. Lacy put the raincoat in the hall closet and the lilacs in a bowl and during the day she frequently leaned down to smell the lilacs and if anyone had watched her they would have seen a smile on her face every time she did this.

That night Lacy and Paul went to a dinner party. Lacy was a little startled when she walked in and saw that Tom and his wife Ruth were guests too. Tom greeted Lacy as though he had never seen her in a garden and told her she was a nymph growing from a lilac tree.

After dinner at the bridge table, Tom's wife said as she heard his partner call him for a bad play, "Don't pay much attention to Tom, he's a little mad. Why, when he came in the house last night after midnight I asked him where he had been. Not that I really cared but his shoes were muddy and he was wet, so I thought it would be a nice wifely gesture to show some solicitude, and what do you think he said?

" 'I've been in a garden making love to a nymph.'

"And there he was, holding some lilacs in his hand, looking absolutely looney to me. You know I can't stand lilacs. They remind me of my childhood and my grandfather, who had a lilac garden and who was impossibly strict and severe. But anyway, there was my husband, standing with mud over his shoes and lilacs in his arms, asserting that he had been making love to a nymph. Then he insisted on putting the lilacs in a bowl and sniffing them! Really! Nymphs growing out of a tree!" concluded Ruth.

The guests all laughed; Ruth had such a droll way of saying things and she made up the most preposterous stories.

But Tom leaned over to Lacy's table and asked, "Lacy, Ruth says there are no nymphs growing out of lilac trees. What do you think?"

Lacy put down her cigarette and answered, "I think there are and if these unbelievers had come to our neighbor's garden last night at midnight they would have seen a nymph. As a matter of fact, I heard her talking to you last night."

"Such nonsense," said Ruth. "I bid two clubs."

But Lacy smiled at Tom. There was no doubt that it was mad to go hunting lilacs at midnight, but she knew that for once, at least, she had been a nymph growing from a lilac tree.

"What happened after that?" I asked her after she told me the story.

"What do you think happened? I called Tom at his office to thank him for the coat and then he asked me for lunch, and I'm falling in love with him!"

"What are you going to do about it?"

"God, I don't know," answered Lacy. "I can't bear to cheat and I don't want to tell Paul but I don't want to give up Tom. I suppose we'll muddle along hoping no one finds out about us."

"You will inevitably get in a mess," I told her. But she didn't. The affair has been going on for years.

Tom is happy, so is Lacy, and Paul and Tom's wife are blissfully ignorant of the romance. So all four continue to be happy. And the moral as far as I can see it is that as long as the romance is kept secret all is well, for all four are living a fairy tale and in fairy tales everyone lives happily ever afterward.

Jane Fonda and the Duke of Windsor

Nathaniel Morton kept a record of Plymouth Colony based on the account of the Pilgrims and how they came to the New World as reported by William Bradford, the governor: "So they left that goodly and pleasant city of Leyden, which had been their resting-place for above 11 years, but they knew that they were pilgrims and strangers here below, and looked not much on these things, but lifted up their eyes to Heaven, their dearest country, where God hath prepared for them a city (Heb. 11:16), and therein quieted their spirits.

"When they came to Delfs-Haven they found the ship and all things ready, and such of their friends as could not come with them followed after them, and sundry came from Amsterdam to see them shipt, and to take their leaves of them. They went on board and their friends with them, where truly doleful was the sight of that sad and mournful parting, to hear what sighs and sobs and prayers did sound amongst them; what tears did gush from every eye, and pithy speeches pierced each other's heart, that sundry of the Dutch strangers that stood on the Key as spectators could not refrain from tears. But the tide (which stays for no man) calling them away, that were thus loath to depart, their Reverend Pastor, falling down on his knees, and they all with him, with watery cheeks commended them with the most fervent prayers unto the Lord and His blessing; and then with mutual embraces and many tears they took their leaves one of another."

When at last they finished their journey over that vast ocean and arrived on the bleak coast of Massachusetts, there was no committee to greet them, no Ramada Inn to find warmth and shelter, no hospital to take care of the sick, no neighbors to bring them food—only a vast wilderness of forest and thicket, animals, and hostile Indians. They were completely on their own—a mighty ocean separated them from all they had known, and now they must learn to survive sustained by their dreams of freedom and their own courage. Never did a handful of people face a more difficult task, to build shelter and provide food, and to face a forbidding continent.

The world of America was made by the adventurer, the dreamer, the malcontent, the individualists, those who were willing to face hunger and cold for a conviction. It became a tradition. Our heroes were those who, to sustain their convictions, were willing to pay the price of public disapproval—the Johnny Appleseeds, Thoreau, the Freeholders, Thomas Paine, the Mormons, and those against slavery, and dozens of others.

They had not lived in a wilderness in Europe nor were they hunters or fishers of food. No life style was waiting for them to fit into; they had to create their own. But they brought with them dreams and convictions, and only those with similar dreams followed them to the new land. Indentured servants came who cried out for freedom. Aristocrats came also with dreams of wealth, of power, and left the "old country" with disdain for the tyrannies and governments they disapproved of.

One thing they all had in common, their courage, their stamina, and resourcefulness, which guaranteed their safety and very existence. In time they moved westward into the wilderness where there were no next-door neighbors whose judgments would influence their conduct. As a result, they became the most individualistic of any people. They were individuals in the most literal sense of the word. An amazing independence of spirit and mind became a gift which their children inherited. It is a magnificent gift and though it very often imposes a price on the inheritors, it remains a priceless gift for any nation.

I thought of this heritage when I interviewed Jane Fonda. Whether you approve of what she stands for or not she is an independent spirit. When she came to Cleveland, she was stopped at the airport and her bags examined. She was suspected of bringing in dope because her bag had a great quantity of pills. Actually, chemical analysis proved them to be vitamins. She protested and was forced into a room where she was detained. She was allowed one call to her attorney. He called her back but she was denied the right to talk to him. So that he would know that she was being held, she burst into the *"Marseillaise"* at the top of her lungs. She was carrying some tapes of interviews she had made with GI's; they were confiscated without any legal right.

I interviewed her in the lobby of the jail surrounded by reporters. She had just been released. Here she told me her story—she had been held in some room at the airport for four hours. She wanted to go to the bathroom and a policeman blocked her way. She pushed him and he yelled, "Did you see that? She attacked me. You're under arrest for assault and battery."

She was handcuffed and stripped and searched by a policewoman and then taken to jail. It was when she was released from jail that I talked with her. I offered her a change of clothes if she needed any or anything else I might be able to provide. The fact is that none of the charges stuck—neither the accusation of assault and battery or the pills. They were exactly what she said they were—vitamins—and the policeman would have had trouble persuading the judge that she was a physical menace to the officer, for she doesn't weigh much over 115 pounds. What was her sin? What crime had she committed? She was against the Vietnamese war passionately and stubbornly; she even found merit in the North Vietnamese and she was obstreperously vocal about how she felt.

Did this experience break her? To the contrary she continued to talk against the war and when she ran out of money, she went back to the movies and won an Oscar for her brilliant performance of a call girl in *Klute*. She is a conscientious craftswoman and before she played the role she managed to acquaint herself with some of the New York City prostitutes so that her interpretation would be realistic.

The second time I talked with her was in October of 1973. She had with her her baby son—four or five months old. Her eldest child, Vanessa, was frequently taken with her on her journey around the country. The baby needed a change of diapers (the operation was performed in my office) and I'm sure that such a scene is never likely to take place again in my office—Jane Fonda and the nurse taking care of the infant's needs. She was divorced from Roger Vadim and married to Tom Hayden, the father of the infant boy. Immediately after the change of diapers we went into the TV studio where the interview took place. She has her followers and sympathizers but letters to the editor all over the country berated her; one outraged congressman even wanted her arrested for treason; the indignation was particularly great when she evinced sympathy for the North Vietnamese.

Whether one approves of her or is alienated by her support of the so-called Left and her attitude toward the war, particularly journeying to North Vietnam where, of course, she was enthusiastically welcomed because she was against the war, the fact remains that she is one of that rare group of dissenters who will pay any price for their convictions. It is the dissenter, the rebel, that creates chaos but who also opens new paths for those of us who support the establishment, the majority, who have neither the desire nor the courage for change.

It is part of the American heritage hidden away in our genes, the capacity to light a star for ourselves and follow it.

I pointed out to Miss Fonda that the attention she receives is not so much for her convictions as it is for the fact that a famous movie star is involved in an anti-war crusade. She admitted that this was so and also freely said she was willing to use every asset to achieve her goal.

"Why," I asked her, "do you do this? You could lead a comfortable life. Why don't you go back to the theater?"

"I have plans to do that but first I must help obtain the release of the political prisoners in Vietnam."

"The case consumes you, doesn't it?" I asked.

"Yes," was her reply. "I can't sit by and see injustice done."

"But you could have an easy, luxurious life as a famous movie star."

She shrugged her shoulders. "We all obey our destiny." And this cause was a burden she had assumed.

In my office her son lay peacefully sleeping because he was dry and had been fed. Perhaps that is all of our hungers equated in simple words—we want to be dry and fed.

To see her dressed in slacks and a sweater instead of furs and jewels, which we generally associate with movie stars, is startling, but only adds to her unusual attitude to society and our life style.

The truth is that the majority of Americans were against the war, not only because it was destroying millions of acres of land and killing thousands and thousands and costing billions but above all what were we doing in Vietnam? If we had wanted to stop the communists, the place should have been Czechoslovakia.

Here was a young woman who had everything—family, breeding, fame, money, looks. Why would she expose herself to jail arrest, censure, and disapproval? This is the mystery, the power of an idea, a conviction. It is the glory of the human mind and heart that there are those who are willing to pay any price to maintain the integrity of their convictions. It takes extraordinary courage—a price is always enacted by society for those who differ loudly and articulately with the accepted action.

It's the non-conformist who gives color to history. The Duke of Windsor defied a thousand years of tradition to give up his throne for love. Other kings and rulers loved women but never gave up their thrones for them. To be king was to be all powerful, the pomp and glory were intoxicating. Why give it up? Louis XIV had a queen but he had mistresses. Charles II had a queen but also the fascinating Nell Gwynne; Carol had a queen but loved Magda. So intoxicated were we with the glory of kingship that to hear a king of a mighty empire (that was before the Second World War—when England was the mightiest empire in the world) announce in noble words that rather than give up the woman he loved, he would abdicate his throne, literally shook the world. Mrs. Simpson was no virgin maid. This was a twice-divorced woman of the world. Would she not have been content to be his mistress? As his mistress she would have been accepted by English society but, of course, in royal circles she would have been accorded no royal status. He was too proud to offer her such a relationship. Why did he make this sacrifice? And afterward, through the long years when neither the English nor any society ever made any demands on him, did he ever regret it?

Did she ever wonder if the price he paid was too great? What could he do to give some purpose to life? He had no profession—being trained to be a king doesn't equip one for anything else. Were there not great hours of boredom for both?

What did she have that made his love for her so great, beyond most loves? Was it her wit? Was it her ability to laugh and be gay or was the passion of sex between them so unique that all other women became insignificant? If she was no virgin maid, neither was he inexperienced in relationships with women. The emotion he felt in his courtship of her must have been very moving. His was the sacrifice to achieve their marriage, for her there was no sacrifice.

The world thrilled at the romance—the greatest in this century—and for generations to come the tellers of tales and dramatists will keep the story alive. Helen of Troy, for whose sake a thousand ships were launched, has not had more poems and tales written about her than will the Duchess of Windsor, who now sits frail and ill and lonely in the house which the Duke and she built. Perhaps she stops by his room each night to say, "And so good night, sweet prince, for all the days to come."

The Duke was a man of great urbanity. Probably the most aristocratic of all the men whom I have met professionally. To obtain an interview with him I used the technique which is always the most successful—the direct and honest approach. When my director couldn't get through to him on the telephone (he and the Duchess were at the Waldorf Astoria in New York City), I tried, and unaware that I was talking to the Duke (I thought it was the butler or the secretary answering), I explained that I would like to interview the Duke for two reasons: I admired him enormously and thought he was the most romantic figure of his generation and besides I was honest enough to tell him that it would be the scoop of the year.

"But," he answered laughingly, "I am the Duke, and who are you?"

You can imagine my consternation and embarrassment, but he consented to come and appear on my show. However, he would appear only if all the questions and answers were written out on a teleprompter. The questions were not significant. I couldn't ask the questions I really wanted to, such as "Why do you love the Duchess so much? What magic does she have? Aren't you very rich?"

After all, the Windsor family is fantastically rich. They own vast areas of valuable land, mines, stocks, paintings, and jewels whose worth can't be calculated.

"Why didn't you stick it out? Ultimately, you would have won over the English people?"

But I didn't; I asked inane and harmless questions. We talked about his book, which had just been released, and about the world situation at that moment. He was obviously nervous about the interview and rehearsed it a number of times. This is the only time of the thousands of interviews I have done that there was a rehearsal of any questions decided on beforehand. I would not conduct an interview if I were not familiar enough with the subject to discuss it. As a professional I am supposed to be competent to discuss the subject at hand. When it was over, he turned to me with the same enthusiasm I show to my dentist when the filling of a tooth is accomplished with no pain.

"Well," he said, "it wasn't painful at all. I wouldn't mind doing this with you often." If he had only known it, I would have been delighted to have another opportunity to be with him any time, anywhere.

"Do you do this kind of thing frequently?" he asked.

"Of course," I answered, "every day."

"Why?" he asked.

"To pay the rent," I told him.

He looked at me startled and then smiled and said, "I'm delighted you have to or I wouldn't have had this pleasure of meeting you."

Obviously, I was enraptured. It isn't often that a king, even a former king, complimented me. He charmed the entire crew by going around and shaking hands with them. No present member of the English royal family has equaled him in personal charm; his deportment and manners were impeccable.

There is a rough and tumble quality to our manners today. Gone is the elegance and distinction of conduct that added so much to our life style. In addition, the late Duke of Windsor had the spirit and the courage to do what he deemed right. Whether he was wise or not in his decision is beside the point. He was one of the rare ones doing what he decided, though it was against all custom and tradition. No woman ever had a greater tribute paid to her than the Duchess of Windsor, but how sad that his life was so useless and that he found no avenue for adventure and performance.

Six Days

In the last days of May the lilacs lost their perfume and withered away and the first days of June saw the roses begin their blooming into an uncomparable beauty and the tender greens turn into the deeper and richer tones; and when in Israel wild mustard and lavender thistle covered the meadows and the valleys, Egypt began her encirclement of Israel. Egypt closed the Gulf of Aqaba, King Hussein decided to ignore the insults hurled at him for months, journeyed to Egypt, embraced Nasser and vowed eternal brotherhood; this seal of brotherhood was applauded by Ahmad Asaad Shukairy of the Palestinian organization. Also an Iraqi unit joined the Egyptian army poised in Sinai, Kuwait sent an infantry brigade to join the Egyptians, and King Faisal of Saudi Arabia contributed twenty thousand soldiers. The might of the Arab world was united—pledged not to defeat but to annihilate the state of Israel.

The world watched with horror. Not a voice was raised by any nation or government to aid Israel; her doom seemed imminent. The blossoming flowers might well have become a funeral wreath for Israel.

David slew Goliath because he was adroit enough to force the giant to face the sun, thus blurring his vision. So the Israelis met the Arab giant with superior planning and thought.

I had been in Israel immediately after the war in 1948. I had been in Egypt and Israel in 1956. In May 1967, it was obvious that war was inevitable and that once more men would die. I was eager to go to Israel, for I knew it was a historic moment. But no one could have envisioned the drama that was to take place in the Middle East early in June, lasting for six days—an unparalleled six days, unique in ancient times as well as in the modern world. Its drama, its brilliance, its extraordinary ending was foreseen by no one.

Reluctantly, the manager of WEWS, the television station with which I have been connected for over twenty-five years, agreed to my going to Israel.

"I'm not keen about your going. You're not very prudent, cautious, and you're not twenty years old," he told me.

All facts which could not be denied, but my instinct told me this was to be a clash of unbelievable events.

"Look," I told him, "if you had been manager of a TV station in Cleopatra's time, would you have refused to allow your news analyst to cover the Battle of Actium in which Cleopatra and Marc Antony were defeated and which changed the map of the world?" He wasn't impressed by that argument, but my persistence wore him down.

"All right. You will make a fine target with your red hair. We'd better send someone along who will be a strong escort and help to guard you."

I was enchanted. I had covered many events, traveled to the corners of the earth, without any escort or companion. No one had ever worried about me. This was great. I was to receive M.C! (M.C. stands for "massive coddling.")

"Who have you in mind to accompany me?" I asked.

One of the salesmen, standing around and listening to the conversation, offered his two cents' worth: "Why not a prize fighter?"

"Fine," I retorted, "but I want him good-looking, no cauliflower ears! Also, he must be bright."

"Where can you find a bright prize fighter?"

"That," I retorted, "is not my problem, it's yours. I'm prepared to go alone. And, incidentally, I not only want him good-looking and bright but distinguished. I'm not going to cover a war with an undistinguished escort."

I was an unreasonable woman but they knew by that time I had made my point and was going no matter what the objections were.

As my position grew stronger, my demands became greater. Someone came up with the name of the famous ballplayer Al Rosen, who had played third base with the Indians and is now a vice-president with a well-known security company. Third baseman meant no more to me than first baseman. I think baseball is a dull, slow game when the batter or the pitcher—whatever he is called—stands there with the bat in his hand making up his mind what to do; I could eat a whole sandwich. Unless baseball becomes a faster game, it will lose out to football. It's almost as slow a game as chess. But Mr. Rosen proved to be a delightful companion. That's the way to cover a war. He arranged for cars and permits, and fulfilled all the requirements—strong, good-looking, prestigious, smart, we became good friends and continue so to this day.

We flew to Tel Aviv and arrived at the ungodly hour of one-thirty in the morning. With the exception of a dozen men in uniform—paratroops wearing the green beret—the airport, which is usually crowded with people, was empty. One of the soldiers was six-foot-two, carried a swagger stick, and had the most beautiful golden beard that ever decorated the face of a man. I took one look at him, turned to Al Rosen, and whispered, "Buy him for me."

What an army! The most egalitarian in recorded history, it took every able-bodied man. They arrived in camp in their milk trucks, their own cars, in taxicabs, on their bicycles, or on foot. The Boy Scouts delivered the mail, all the mailmen were in the Army. When I phoned the desk for room service, a polite voice answered, "Sorry, madam, we have no room service. All our waiters are in the Army."

The Israeli Army had sixty thousand regulars, two hundred thousand reservists of a population of two and a half million. It was not an army of spit and polish. It was an army that looked shabby, that wasn't properly dressed. There was no thirty- to sixty-day mobilization period, the war was on them with little notice.

General Abraham Yaffe reported an incident that could happen only in an egalitarian army. Early in the battle he heard a soldier ask permission to take a route other than the one his platoon had been directed to take because he told his commanding officer, "I see a bunch of Arab tanks over there, and I think we ought to take them."

"I told him," the general said, "to stick his nose into his own business and not interfere with others."

The point was they kept trying to find their own individual enemy and destroy him.

The Army was small and the Israelis had to be inventive. One story was of an officer who captured a contingent of Arabs but did not want to use too many of his men to guard them so an order was issued that all the captured men were to drop their belts. They were then collected and destroyed—the idea being that a man whose trousers keep falling down can't run very fast to escape. Even if the story is apocryphal, it is illustrative of how the egalitarian army reverted to just plain common sense to solve unexpected problems.

Nasser was sure of victory, as I wrote in my book *Where Were the Arabs?* He had the most modern armament in the world; he had the Arab countries with him, Russia as his ally, and no other nation except Holland was willing to incur Arab enmity and help Israel. Even De Gaulle was on his side. Victory was to be his; how could he fail? But destiny was preparing to record an astonishing event, for on that fateful June day the sun rose on a sight perhaps never before witnessed by man. On that June morning with skies of brilliant orange and yellow, an Israeli plane took off every twenty seconds. All the radios were silent; they did not want Egypt to hear the communications between the fliers. The Israeli co-ordination was perfect. The pilots were seated in their planes, their watches synchronized; at twenty-second intervals they took off and in three hours had paralyzed twenty-five airfields.

The Egyptian Air Force was totally destroyed. With the accuracy of birds winging to their nests, the Israeli pilots—husbanding their ammunition, ignoring the wooden dummies placed among the real planes—went unerringly to the Egyptian planes. Faster than the swallow flies, they struck, and the blow for victory was delivered. The Arabs had thundered their boasts and warning that no Israeli would be left alive, but it was the Israelis who struck like lightning. Thunder does not do the damage, it is the lightning that destroys and kills.

There was never an air force like this! The Israeli fliers blasted the Arab bases with rockets—and with 30-mm. cannon fire when their bombs were gone. They flew with the speed of lightning; they let go their rockets with precision on the Russian jets lined up so obligingly for them. Not only did they destroy the air armada of the Arabs, given to them by the Russians, but as the Israeli pilots flew into the blue-and-golden sky that June morning, it was as though they had struck the nerve center of the Arabs and paralyzed it, for from that moment the Israelis chalked up one victory after another.

Jerusalem fell and for the first time since the Roman general Titus marched his legions into the Temple to destroy the mysterious God of the Jews, the Jews returned to Jerusalem. But Titus, pulling the curtains aside that covered the Holy of Holies shrine, found no craven image of a god, no statue that he could smash and destroy; for here in the Holy of Holies was the ark and in it the covenant between God and the Jews—the Ten Commandments, an agreement between God and the Jews that they would regulate their relationship with man by their relationship with God. Nineteen centuries later, when the Star of David flew over Jerusalem, there was an outpouring of emotion that swept all of Israel. Men wept unashamedly; Jerusalem the Golden was theirs.

I walked through the streets of Old Jerusalem haunted by the feeling that in no other city in the world had such majestic and noble events taken place—events that had shaped the character, the tradition, the morals, and the religion of the Western world. Here the Savior and His disciples had walked. Believer or non-believer, it is a fact that here and here alone in the whole world had a Man arisen Who became for untold millions their interceder with God for their immortality. He, like all the biblical figures were Jews, and this day shaken by events I walked through the streets strewn with broken glass and stones, rubble from the Six Day War—for it was another act in the drama of Jerusalem.

My photographer was with me, and we stopped to examine an apartment house that had been shelled. The shrapnel holes were very visible. I stopped and had my photographer take some pictures of the damaged building. While doing this I noticed a woman hanging up her laundry. Startled, I said, "Do you wash your clothes in wartime?"

She shrugged her shoulders. "Because Nasser has to have a war every ten years, my family should go dirty?" Then, putting her hands on her hips, she said, "I hope he has a headache for another ten years and lets us alone."

I smiled and began walking away. She called out, "Miss America, come back!" The inaccuracy of that title didn't bother me. I never had been saluted by that complimentary description; I enjoyed it. So, I turned back to where she was standing.

"Look at my laundry," she commanded, "what do you think?"

"What about it?"

With an ironic smile she answered, "Don't you see it dries faster because now I get the breeze from Old Jerusalem as well as New Jerusalem?"

These are a sturdy people with a robust as well as ironic sense of humor.

I drove over to the municipal building and took the elevator to the mayor's office. Teddy Kollek exclaimed when he saw me (I had interviewed him on my show some years before when he was in Cleveland), "What are you doing here?"

"Oh," I answered nonchalantly, "I happened to be in town so I thought I would drop in."

He grinned and said, "How would you like to see my town?"

I climbed to the top of the municipal building and looked down on Jerusalem and up into the sky. No member of Western culture with its heritage of biblical figures could help but be moved, for I realized that that same sky had looked down upon Jesus, the disciples, Abraham, Ruth, Peter, Pontius Pilate, Mary.

The taking of Jerusalem was a bloody affair, house-to-house fighting. Before the city fell to Israel, a thousand Israeli homes had been pounded by mortar shells. Within a week after the war, Kollek's city government was repairing windows and doors that had been shot out. These Israelis are a pragmatic, efficient people with an intellectual equipment that guarantees their survival.

Long before they had an army they built a university. They are a people of "The Book"—a people of learning and determination. Through a long and agonizing past, they have been chiseled into strength against adversity. For the persecution, subtle as well as violent, they have suffered through the ages. Strong and ingenious, inventive and sturdy, they have built a life in a hostile environment.

It was unbelievable . . . the emotion that was aroused by the fall of Jerusalem. A thousand thousand Israelis poured out to stand before the Wailing Wall, men wept and embraced strangers. For two thousand years they had dreamed of this day. For two thousand years they had wandered and left their agony and grief in a hundred countries. Now they had come home, as Teddy Kollek told me. "Jerusalem the Golden, let me be the harp that sings thy song," was their litany; but the Israeli victory had been no guarantee for peace.

Nasser had become drunk with his own wine. He had begun to believe his own nonsense: that the Arab countries could survive only if Israel were destroyed; that Arab unity was dependent upon the destruction of Israel. This became his theme song, his litany.

If an individual conducted himself in such an absurd fashion, he would be described as insane. Israel does not have any natural resources; she has no oil, no gold. Land? The Arabs have millions of acres that are uninhabited and not used. Is the Israeli land more valuable than the Arab? It's made of rock and desert, but the Israelis have conquered the land by their sweat and their toil. They knew they had to conquer the desert or the desert would swallow them. What then have the Israelis that the Arabs covet? How can two and a half million people be a menace to a hundred million? Eight thousand square miles is as nothing compared to the vast areas of the Arab world. What nonsense to maintain that Israel is a menace. One would imagine that the Arabs would be too proud to admit that they are afraid of a handful of Jews. Nasser was too smart not to be cognizant of this fact.

Where was the world's sense of humor? Two and a half million people—a threat to one hundred million? The idea should have been laughed at and the Arabs should have been told that their attitude was ridiculous and absurd.

Our last night in Israel Al Rosen and I joined a group of foreign correspondents in the bar at the Hilton in Tel Aviv. The bartender had returned from the Army and shrugged his shoulders when I asked for his story.

"The story," he said, "has only two words—we survived."

"But you war guys are all heroes!" I exclaimed.

He looked at me quizzically.

"Lady," he said, "it's nice to win, but you know what? I like tending bar better."

I Hate Eggs

I am a hyperglycemia victim. I'm supposed to eat eggs and bacon for breakfast because they are proteins, but I hate eggs. I loathe every hen that produces them. If I want to give myself nightmares, all I have to do is envision the millions and millions of cackling hens—all potential producers of eggs.

If they are soft-boiled, the yolks offend my aesthetic sense. For no matter how daintily one eats the yolk it invariably leaves a rim on either one's lips or the napkin. The white part has no character, no taste, no flavor.

Contrast an egg with a gingersnap. A fresh gingersnap crackles and breaks into lovely firm pieces. It has character. Also, it has a delicate aroma with a decisive flavor somewhere between an apricot and a sunflower with a dash of ginger. Who can describe accurately and poetically the pleasure of a "dunked" gingersnap? Only the unknowing, the unsophisticated palate will eat an "undunked" gingersnap.

A tall cup of French coffee—half hot milk and half coffee—according to my calculations is needed for the dunking of seven gingersnaps. What greater delight than to sit at the breakfast table with the morning paper and dip the gingersnaps into the warm coffee.

Do not imagine that this can be done dexterously without practice, for it is necessary not to leave the gingersnap in the coffee too long otherwise it will break up and become part of the coffee. The trick is to bring the dunked cookie to one's lips while it is still whole. I've figured I can dally fifteen seconds from the time the cookie is dipped in the coffee until it reaches my mouth intact. Then, what a lovely, lively, agitated, stimulated taste.

I've read Walter Lippmann, Evans and Novak, Alsop, Jack Anderson, Dear Abby, all to the rhythm of dunking gingersnaps. My granddaughter, observing me one morning eating my breakfast, heard her mother say, "You are supposed to eat proteins, not gingersnaps." My granddaughter, whose vocabulary has been molded in patterns which she hears, looked up from her book and said with quiet elegance, "Why don't you say to hell with proteins, Grandma?"

"Spoken," I said to myself, "with wisdom."

An ode to the neglected gingersnap that has given me more pleasure than caviar and champagne served on a candle-lighted dinner table.

A Roman Fountain

Taffy Georgetown and I were friends of long standing. We had been very close at college, having dated two brothers, and through the years we had kept in contact. I was a bridesmaid at her wedding and marched down the aisle feeling as self-conscious as all bridesmaids do. Her marriage lasted only five years and some years later she married George Georgetown. She married him, she asserted, because of his ridiculous name.

"Imagine," she said, "how clerks look at me when I say, 'Send it to Mrs. George Georgetown.'"

The marriage was a happy one and after her husband's early retirement at fifty-five years of age they decided to live in Europe for a year savoring the foods of various countries in order to write a gourmet cookbook. After doing this in a leisurely way for over a year, they decided to buy a villa in Rome and travel from there as the spirit moved them. It was an ideal arrangement except that their life was so leisurely that writing the book became a task, so they very wisely decided that the hedonists had something and gave up the idea of doing anything creative, resigning themselves with no sighs to enjoying their days. Which decision, of course, made them eager and delightful hosts.

When Taffy and her husband finally settled in Rome, I was invited to visit them. This became a routine. Both Taffy and her husband were very cordial and I came to visit at their villa frequently.

Arriving in Rome one July day, I phoned to say I was in town and was promptly invited to come up immediately. After doing some more phoning and unpacking, I walked down the Via Veneto past the Excelsior Hotel. Hopping in a cab, I was driven to their villa, which was situated on a hill surrounded by olive trees.

The maid informed me that I would find Mrs. Georgetown in the kitchen, where she and Maria, the cook, were shelling peas. The Georgetowns were gourmets and no frozen peas were in their larder even if they were available in Rome.

Taffy was sitting at the table pulling the pods apart and rolling the peas into a leaf-lined basket. She rose to greet me with her usual warmth and pulled a chair out for me. Maria, a dark, dour-looking woman, was also seated at the table chopping parsley into small bits. I had met Maria many times and usually went out in the kitchen to say hello to her and inquire about her son. If there was a husband, I never heard about him, but Maria would talk a great deal about her boy, who was eleven years of age. Not that I understood everything she said, but she seemed to enjoy talking about her son. According to Taffy, the boy had no father, at least no one who admitted to being his progenitor. Maria had left the little village where she grew up and had come to Rome to have her baby. She had a tough time and worked two jobs—one at the airport and weekends for Taffy.

"How are you, Maria?" I asked.

"You know, this is Maria's last day with us," Taffy said.

"How come?" I inquired of Maria, whose English was about equal to my Italian vocabulary of a hundred words. It is a pity that I never pursued the language because Italian is musical. The vowels are pronounced and it has some of the purity of Latin in its grammar and form.

Maria turned to Taffy with a smile and said, "You tell."

"Maria," explained Taffy, "is rich and isn't going to work any more."

I looked my surprise. Maria worked for Taffy only on weekends. Her regular job was that of attendant for the women's washroom at the enormous airport in Rome. Since people of all nations come through the airport Maria's tips were coins of many nations and once a week she would tie the coins in a large handkerchief, take them to the money exchange window, and turn them in for lire. Between that and the weekend work for Taffy she lived in what could be described as a sub-modest fashion with her son. In any event, Maria had come into some money and was going back to the village where she was born to buy some land and live.

"Who gave her the money? Did she inherit it?" I inquired.

Taffy, who had finished the shelling, said, "Come and sit on the terrace. Everything is in bloom and we can overlook the city while we talk."

The villa was perched high on a hill and commanded a good if not spectacular view of the city, which does have a golden quality. For anyone who is familiar with the history of Rome, from the legend of mighty Caesar, who loved Cleopatra long enough to stay with her in Alexandria until their child was born, to the days when Michelangelo hurled his titanic figures on the Sistine ceiling, to the present day of Roman café life, Rome is forever fascinating. To explain the lure of Rome is like trying to explain why certain people have charm—charisma as is the popular way of describing it. Cities have personalities just as human beings do. London is a man's city, aristocratic, elegant, and dressed in evening clothes. San Francisco is a twenty-five-year-old young woman, with hair streaming in the wind, driving a convertible. New York City is a carnival and a theater and the future. Tokyo is like a family reunion in too small a house. Paris is a woman no longer young, but with infinite beauty and perfume, walking on a fall day. Rome is gold, golden—a Renaissance painting of a golden-haired woman, full-bosomed, with half-lowered eyelids, remembering many things.

"To explain Maria's sudden fortune I have to go back a number of years. Do you remember," asked Taffy, "at a dinner some years ago meeting Count Rudolpho and his wife, Dolores? You must remember her. She was very beautiful, with hair that really did look like spun gold and eyes the color of an azure sky."

"Yes," I answered, "but she seemed so remote I never got up enough courage to start a conversation with her."

"You know," she told me, "Dolores was a Philadelphia girl of a good family but of limited income. When Dolores was eighteen her schooling was over. Her parents had just enough money for a modest coming-out party, which was held in early December. Among the guests was an Italian who was in Philadelphia on business and was visiting one of Dolores' parents' friends. He was the Count Rudolpho whom you met. He was young and dashing and was apparently enchanted with Dolores' beauty and a certain quality of fragility and purity. She was undeniably lovely to look at and the Count was undeniably in love. It was a whirlwind courtship and Dolores fell madly in love with the Count. Whether he thought the family has a good deal of money no one knows. But the young girl's beauty and the passionate love she evinced apparently were enough for the Count. Her family were not too happy. It meant a separation from Dolores, whose beauty had added to her mother and father's pride. In addition to their paternal affection, there was the added sense of having something special in Dolores and her extraordinary beauty. In two months she was married and he carried her off to Rome."

Fate was, if one can so describe fate, perverse, for Dolores grew to believe that it was her beauty that engaged the Count's passion for her. She must, therefore, never lose that beauty. So she began to exercise all of her interest and effort on preserving her loveliness. And she was lovely. Many words were used by her admirers to describe her rare loveliness. Her eyes were blue, the blue of sunlit skies. Her hair was neither blond nor red but the color of golden red and her skin of rare delicacy. But mostly it was the bone structure of her face with a nose that looked as though it had been chiseled by some plastic surgeon to superlative perfection. Her smile was enchanting and at the corner of her lip a tiny mole emphasized the pure lines of her lips. Add to that a graceful figure, which she carried with a slight sway, and you could understand why Roman newspapers described her as the incarnation of a Botticelli painting. She was photographed over and over in periodicals, magazines, and society columns.

She had always known she was beautiful, for she had always been told so. A doting father and mother had not realized that Dolores the little girl, told so often that she was lovely to look at, began to feel that being beautiful was a virtue, that being beautiful meant she was a good child pleasing her mother and father.

As a child she heard constantly, "What a beautiful little girl," at which her mother smiled and petted her. Her father kissed her. Being beautiful made them love her more.

"Tell me, little one, where did you steal the blue for your eyes? From the sky?"

"Look at that child's hair. It looks like spun gold."

"Come here, little one," and Dolores, being an obedient child, would come and a grown-up would stroke her hair and say to the mother, "She looks like angels are supposed to look."

In school it was the same thing—"Enchanting Dolores, lovely Dolores, exquisite Dolores." At high school Dolores was never without a date. Every prom, every dance brought the invitations. Not that Dolores said much. She smiled and that seemed to be enough. She never was obliged to learn to be good company or to be a friend or to engage in necking. Her beauty and her fragility kept the boys from any physical advances. Even kissing was very rare. She knew that boys were supposed to be wolves but something about Dolores kept them at arm's length. They showered her with adulation. "How lovely," "Boy, are you beautiful," "Honey, you are a real dish," "Gosh, are you something," "Don't tell me you are real," "Where, you lovely creature, did you come from?" "I say, Botticelli must have used you for a model," "I didn't know there was any living creature as beautiful as you." Unconsciously, without being aware of it, the adulation she received, the acclaim for her beauty, became a necessity. When she was little it made her parents love her more. As she grew older, "Dolores, you are beautiful," became as necessary to her as food. Her entire thoughts and plans were centered around her beauty.

She loved the Count and the Count, enthralled by her beauty, turned his love-making into a paean of praise for her beauty. Dolores had had no experience with sex before her marriage. She had no way of expressing it. She never approached her husband, always waited for him to start a physical encounter. But always, his demand for her was when she looked particularly beautiful. It was then that the Count would exclaim, "*Mamma mia*, Dolores, you are more beautiful than roses, stars, sunshine, everything combined." And Dolores, shy and restrained, would deny him nothing, but she was a taker of passion not a giver and it was inevitable that the Count would do some wandering. This, after all, was in the 1940s. This was still the period where there were two codes for sex behavior, one for the male, where latitude was expected, and the other, purity for women.

For Dolores, the Count's love-making was the result of her beauty. It was the tribute to her beauty and it became a necessity to hear exclamations of admiration for her looks. It became sustenance, her reason for being. It prompted her to appear constantly, at one function after another, in an endless array of gorgeous garments. She was the cynosure of all eyes when she and the Count went anywhere and the Count enjoyed having his wife the queen of beauty; she was his possession. Dolores, for her part, waited eagerly for the Count's tribute, his warm and passionate embraces, while he extolled her beauty.

It was inevitable that she became the slave of her beauty. The fear that relentless time, the irreversibility of time, might mar her looks began to haunt Dolores. The fear engulfed and imprisoned her. To ward off the possible marring by time of her extraordinary looks, hours of the day were spent in massages, cream potions to rest the eyes, cream for the feet, massage for the hands, treatment for the hair, exercise for the body. Practically every day some photographer had an appointment with Dolores. Every reporter wanted to do a story about the Countess. Every benefit wanted the Countess to be the honorary chairman because that automatically guaranteed them publicity. So Dolores spent more and more hours in preserving her beauty and appearing at various functions. To appear at this luncheon or that dinner became like wine or a drug. She needed the acclaim, the articulated appreciation of her looks. She was drunk with the excitement her appearance always produced and it became a necessity greater than any other need.

The dedicated hours began to interfere with the Count's desire for Dolores. Too frequently he found the Countess either had an appointment with her masseuse or with some magazine for pictures. It was not as he had pictured a marriage. It was all well and good for his wife's beauty to be acclaimed but not at the expense of the serenity of their marriage. She was his wife and he should come first—before appointments, social affairs, etc.

"How beautiful you are, Dolores, and tonight you made every woman appear dull and colorless compared to you." Such words would win Dolores and she would willingly come to his arms and to his bed. But what Dolores wanted was his passion coated with words describing her beauty. The Count on the other hand was not always poetical. Sometimes it was desire unadorned and not verbal. At such times Dolores endured but did not return his passion. The Count wanted a child, but Dolores shrank from the thought of a pregnancy which would distort her figure. Adulation, admiration for her beauty, had become a necessity. Not only did she hunger for worship of her beauty by the Count, but she herself began to worship her loveliness. It was a true case of narcissism. She watched her Botticelli beauty and her slim body and fled to a doctor to equip her with what was necessary to prevent conception. Now her figure was safe. Now the elegant slimness of her legs and swaying body would be preserved.

Now there were hours devoted to massages and creaming of that fragile and camellia-like skin. Her house was run with the same elegance and beauty because it was a background for her own appearance. The appointments were exquisite so that her own body and face were enhanced.

One night at a dinner the Count watched Dolores, who was dressed in white. "My God," he thought, "how beautiful my wife really is. But does she feel anything? Her fear of becoming pregnant keeps her from me and I am beginning to feel as though I were married to an icicle. I am ready for an adventure with someone perhaps less lovely, but more earthy and with more passion."

For the Count to contemplate a sexual encounter with another woman validated its possibility. And it was Dolores who walked into the library to find the Count in the act of kissing one of her friends with abandon and excitement. He had not seen her, and she was too proud to discuss it with her husband but it froze her passion. Some days later when he found her sitting in front of her dressing table, he lifted her hair from her shoulders and began to kiss her arms, but she moved away from him.

"You are my wife, are you not? Why do you draw away from me?"

Dolores, unable to say because I saw you making love to another woman, too proud to upbraid him, answered, "I am tired and my masseuse is waiting for me." Her husband turned on his heel and walked out of the room.

A series of such episodes alienated them further and Dolores began hearing stories of his infidelities.

Her pride wounded, she was subconsciously convinced it was her beauty that would restore the Count's fidelity to her. But the Count was promiscuous by nature and even if Dolores had returned his passion he would have exercised his masculinity by wooing and apparently always winning a number of women.

He recognized Dolores' enchanting and ethereal loveliness. He was delighted to have his wife the object of universal admiration. He never denied her anything. Her wardrobe was fabulous. She was his decoration, his jewel. But the hours she spent to preserve her beauty alienated him. He would have infinitely preferred her less lovely but more earthy and the mother of his children, but since that was impossible he was quite capable of appreciating many women. And women appreciated the Count. Why not? He was good-looking, gay, charming, and spent money. He would kiss Dolores' lovely white hands and then go out seeking hands that were not so white, so delicate, but hands that clasped his body with ardent desire.

Now her life and days became a ritual of preserving her beauty. As long as she was beautiful she was sure Rudolpho would never leave her. Hours were spent in preparing herself for any event. She waited for the moment when she joined him to hear him say, "You are without doubt the most beautiful woman in all of Rome." If he no longer loved her with passion, she was still his possession and he took pride in the admiration she elicited wherever she went. Now when she entertained she did it as an artist preparing a canvas—every detail, from the color of the linens to match the flowers and the flowers to match her shade of lipstick. Her dinners became famous and invitations to them were eagerly sought after. She took to spending a long time deciding on what was to be served at dinner. No plate was allowed on the table without a trimming of some flower. The wines, chosen for their color as well as their bouquet, were served in jeweled glasses. Guests were enthralled at the attention she gave to such details. Her dining room was perfumed with roses.

She had only to mention something she would like and it was hers. If he no longer gave her passion, he gave her attention and appreciation. He never suggested that she was extravagant.

She never spoke to him of his infidelities. It was as though she refused recognition of a devastating fact. She became more and more impersonal. Her one desire was to keep the wall between them unnoticed by their family or friends. She wanted no sympathy and as the years went on, she became more and more detached from all emotion. Her luxuries were her delight. Her exquisite room in its purple hues. Her drawing room with its soft carpets and fresh flowers. Her furs, sable and ermine, soft and perishable. The perfumes, her pillows, her sheets, the quilts on her bed, all with different scents. To entertain meant the pleasure of handling the delicate linens and the glassware. Dressing was a ritual from the satin foundation garments to the scented gloves. Her smile was radiant, but it belied her, for she felt neither happiness nor unhappiness. She dwelt in a feelingless world and Rudolpho's invariable tributes to her beauty were her only animation. Had Rudolpho been wiser he would have broken down the barriers between them and made Dolores into a wife and human being who had other interests besides her beauty. But the Count was pleasure-loving. He began to find Dolores, though more beautiful than any other woman he had ever seen, a bore. There was little communication between them.

If he had not been a Catholic, he might have sought a divorce. But, as he realized, being married had its compensations. His numerous affairs never could become serious since the various ladies concerned knew he was married.

He was too well bred and even considerate not to keep up the façade of their marriage and hide his infidelities as best he could from Dolores. Dolores knew, but with enormous pride never referred to the Count's philandering.

So the years passed and Dolores was neither happy nor sad. Preserving her ethereal beauty had become the motive of her life. It was her passion. The Count expressed his passions in another fashion.

When Dolores was forty-five years of age Rudolpho died quite suddenly while calling on one of his lady loves.

His lawyers came to see the widow and explained to her that Rudolpho had left a very small estate. He had been living on his capital, selling his land piece by piece, and now there was very little left. If she would live modestly, there was enough to last her lifetime.

"How long would it last on the scale I am used to living?"

"Perhaps five years, no more," they told her.

Dolores thanked them and asked them to instruct the bank to sell everything and deposit the money to her account.

Dolores sat very quietly after they left. Give up the loveliness that surrounded her? The fresh roses and orchids which were brought in daily by the florist? Give up her perfumes, her beauty appointments, live in a tiny flat or *pensione!* Never go to the fashion openings and the adventure of new clothes? This is what life had become—a shrine of beauty where she worshiped with elegance. Rudolpho in death was going to take away the substitute for his love which she had so painstakingly built up through the years.

"No, Rudolpho," she said out loud, "I will not give up my house of worship!"

How many years could she live as she was now living if

she used her capital? Five years did the lawyers say? Perhaps only four if the cost of living went up? Five years of elegance and beauty against a possible ten or fifteen of existence impecunious and bleak.

No change was to take place in her mode of living. She continued to entertain in the same quiet elegant fashion as always and her friends continued to come for the pleasure of the elegance and luxury of her entertaining. Her beauty they said was like cold marble, it must be grief. But it was also obvious that the late Count must have provided for her very well indeed since she lived in the same opulence as she did when he was alive.

The lawyers were alarmed. They asked if they might call and once more pointed out to her how limited the amount of money was that she inherited from her husband.

"Yes, yes," she understood.

Perplexed, the lawyers asked what she would do when the money was exhausted.

"Please, *signori*," said Dolores, "do not worry. I am aware of the limited amount and I am not reckless. I understand and I have plans."

Reassured they left. "Obviously," said one, "she must have an income left to her by her American family."

Dolores made her decision. She would not give up her sybaritical way of life. When the money was gone she would be gone, too, to her eternal sleep. She would not live in unlovely surroundings nor would she give up the accouterments that helped retain her beauty—her masseuse, her hairdresser, her clothes, her beautiful house. She had become, she realized, a drug addict. Without the admiration for her beauty, she was lost, and too late she knew that in her devotion to her beauty she had lost Rudolpho and now everything was too late.

Then came the day when her bank balance was about

five thousand lire. She knew what she had to do. She dismissed her two maids, telling them she would not need them for the weekend.

This last afternoon of her life she ordered her chauffeur to drive through the streets of Rome so that she could take the memory with her through all eternity. She had lately been in the habit of driving by the Trevi Fountain and giving her chauffeur some coins to throw into the water. There were always some Roman youngsters playing around the fountain waiting for some tourists to stop and drop some coins in the bubbling water, for the legend guaranteed return to Rome if coins were dropped in the water. The urchins would reclaim the coins from the water and rush to buy some sweets. She enjoyed watching the youngsters jump into the water to retrieve the coins and rush away to spend their gains.

Before leaving her house, she realized she had no coins for the boys who played around the fountain. Then she recalled a green leather box in her husband's desk in his sitting room in which there were some coins, for he had occasionally collected them. She gave the coins to her chauffeur and instructed him to drive slowly for an hour and to drive by the fountain.

"Throw the coins into the waters of the fountain." She smiled at the youngsters who reclaimed the coins and as they ran with the coins they called out to her, "*Grazie! Grazie!*"

Returning to her villa, she dismissed the chauffeur as she had her other servants. She noticed the day's mail on the table. She shrugged her shoulders. Why read them for she would have no occasion to answer them. But idly she picked one up that bore her solicitor's name. He wrote her that they had received a letter from an Egyptian dealer who many years ago had sold her husband some of his coin collection. Rudolpho had always intended to set up a collection but never quite got round to it. The only coins he had were purchased by him once when he was in Alexandria. In this collection there was a certain coin minted in 1799 in Luxembourg. An American coin collector needed this one particular coin to complete his display and he was offering five million lire for it. If the Countess desired, the lawyers would negotiate the sale, which they said would add a good deal to the Countess's income. Dolores stared at the letter. Then she laughed, for those were the coins she had thrown to the boys in the Trevi Fountain. Well, her rendezvous was not to be interfered with. Destiny had sent her a message.

She perfumed her room with jasmine scent, slowly undressed, put on a gown and negligée, and lay down on her bed, never, of course, to rise again.

Two days later, Roman newspapers carried the story that the Countess was dead in headlines. She had obviously, the report said, mistakenly taken an overdose of sleeping pills.

"One of the urchins," said Taffy, "who played around the fountain was Maria's eleven-year-old and he was lucky that afternoon; diving three times, he picked up nine coins and raced to buy some sweets. The old woman who sold sweets refused to take them, they were not lire and no good for her.

"That night when Maria was washing her son's overalls she found the coins and added them to her collection of coins.

"She took them to the bank and the cashier proceeded to count the American coins, add them, and tabulate the number of lire Maria would receive for them. The same thing was done with the other coins. But when he came to the ancient gold pieces he looked up from his counting.

" 'Maria, I don't know what these nine coins are worth but they are very old, from the seventeenth century, I think. You better take them to some authority on coins; they are probably worth a good deal of money.'

"Maria followed his advice and was able to locate a dealer who found a buyer for the ancient coins. After paying a fee for the services of the dealer, she received enough money so she can go back to her native village and buy some land and a small house. And that's why this is Maria's last day with us," concluded Taffy.

We sat for a while watching the clouds drift by, hearing the buzz of a bee, and reflecting on how strange life could be. I thought of the beautiful Countess who was dead and of Maria, who now could go back to the village in the role of a rich widow and no one but her confessor would know that her wealth was an accident of fate, fate that appears completely indifferent to logic or to justice, completely fortuitous in its pattern.

"But who knows," I said to my hostess, "perhaps if we could see the whole pattern there is a form and a purpose in all the events that form our lives."

"Perhaps," she answered, "but listen to Maria singing. I never heard her sing before." And so I went back into the kitchen to say good-by to Maria and wish her luck.

A Wonderful Engine

Engines in automobiles last only a limited number of years, hearths in steel mills have to be replaced, even copper plumbing wears out, tires have to be replaced, teeth need fillings, eyes fortified with glasses, hair turns gray, but that remarkable, unbelievable organ—the heart—has a spectacular record. Its performance is unbelievable.

Buckminster Fuller probably has the most original unorthodox mind of anyone in the world. He thinks differently from anyone else; for example, he has developed a new timetable. He points out in an article in *World* that healthy hearts beat between 60 and 100 times a minute. You are quite normal if each heartbeat takes a second. In two weeks your heart beats 1,000,000 times; in one year, 26,000,000 heartbeats. You enter college at 550,000,000 heartbeats. At 32, you have had 999,000,000 heartbeats. At 70, you have had 2,130,000,000 heartbeats. Two hundred billion heartbeats ago takes you back 7,000 years. If you go back 2½ million years, when the earliest known humans on earth appeared, and if a heart had been able to beat from that time until today, it would have pulsed 77,-500,000,000,000 times.

Cleopatra died 62,186,000,000 heartbeats ago. The birth of Jesus took place 61,194,000,000 heartbeats ago.

My heart has registered 2,480,000,000 times since my birth. If I live another 10 years, it will have registered 310,000,000 more heartbeats. No engine invented by man could perform as the heart does. It is a magnificent, unmatched engine; and Buckminster Fuller's mind is unmatched for original thinking.

If the heart is an extraordinary muscle, what can one say about the brain?

The miracle of life itself is awesome and so is the infinite variety of techniques developed by nature for the survival of the species. In the Arctic where the temperature falls many degrees below zero, the penguins make a circle, body touching body, thus gathering warmth from each other. To ensure the survival of growing plants, the bee pollinates while gathering the honey for its survival. The beaver builds his dam generation after generation, the pattern always the same. The giant tree spreads its roots deep into the ground raising its swaying branches to the blue of the heavens. How does the crocus know the sun will soon be lavishing its warmth on the earth? How does the robin know it's time to leave the South and come northward? Where did the wild goose learn to fly? Surely the most awe-inspiring art of creation is the universe itself. Is it finite or infinite, never ending? Are the words beginnings and endings useless to describe the vastness of the heavens and the stars they contain?

How did the brain of man develop within 2½ million years to such a degree that though he can see an object at the most perhaps 100 feet away, he has been able to plumb the depths of space by the use of his brain.

Man's brain has transcended the limitations of man's eyesight and has been able from a limited number of clues to describe the vastness of space and how far away the stars are from our planet. So great, so magnificent is the potential of the human brain that it is an intoxicating realization.

The National Academy of Sciences reports that with modern techniques astronomers have discovered stars 100,-000 times brighter than the sun, flickering stars that flare off and on 1,000,000 times a second. Stars whose outbursts of X rays in a single second are 100,000,000,000 times greater than all the electrical power produced by the earth in a year. Stars that whirl at 100 miles per second. Stars that are so densely packed that a piece of the star the size of a lump of sugar weighs as much as all of Manhattan Island. These awesome dimensions of our endless universe are no more awesome than the capacity of the human mind to make these calculations. Creation is releasing its secrets to man! Who can describe the drama of this speck of life in the form of man, an infinite speck in the universe standing on tiptoe to catch the secrets of the stars and the universe itself.

Astronomers have calculated that in 5,000,000,000 years man as well as all animal life will perish because by that time the sun will have become a giant star, no longer a yellow-gold color but red crimson as blood. Its size will have expanded so that it will cover 30 per cent of the sky but by that time no one will be around to be awed and terrified by its size. Life will have disappeared from the planet earth.

Are there other stars with planets that are inhabited or are we the flowering of creation unique and alone in the vastness of space. I doubt that. I believe that there are other planets where conditions prevail that make life possible.

Nature is too profligate with all her species to presume that only with man has she been frugal and limited.

When I stand looking up at the stars, I wonder if there isn't someone like myself standing on some faraway world wondering as I do whether there is life on another planet.

There are those who decry the money we spend on getting to the moon. It's absurd to complain because I believe our urge to go out into space was built into our genes and chromosomes. We could no more control the hunger to reach the moon than we could stop building planes. It was programmed into our being. Man was destined to go into space. This is his supreme reason for being, I believe, and somewhere in space we may meet our God.

It is nonsense to accept as inevitable the deterioration of the brain. The brain is like any other organ—usage develops it. Learning causes the brain to grow. It increases the cerebral cortex, which is the gray matter that constitutes the outer layer of the brain. The older I grow, the faster I assimilate information and the use I make of this erudition is more varied and significant in the editorials which I write daily.

Americans
Are Different

I have a thing about being kept waiting. If I give a dinner party, the evening is spoiled for me if my guests arrive late and the food can't be served at the proper time. It is no longer fashionable to be late to a dinner party; but, obviously, many people that I know are unaware of that.

I'm always on time to the minute. If someone is to pick me up, I'm in the lobby promptly at the appointed time. I get to my seat in the theater so I'm there before the curtain goes up. If the dentist appointment is at two o'clock, I'm there before two. Maybe it's a disease to be so prompt; but when one's day and evening are filled, promptness is the only way one can function.

My husband was always late. I invariably had to wait for him. I used to do a slow burn that could ruin an evening. He was nonchalant about it. "What difference does fifteen or twenty minutes make?" It didn't to him because he was never put out if anyone kept him waiting. He didn't consider promptness a virtue, but a nuisance; and he was baffled by what he called "the tyranny of time."

When Hubert Humphrey was Vice-President, I had occasion to interview him. He kept me waiting for forty minutes. When at last he appeared, I said, "Mr. Vice-President, if you were one of the disciples, I would be annoyed." To appease me he gave me a thin—very thin —gold bracelet with the vice-presidential crest engraved on it. Now, I don't approve of thin gold bracelets. I want them as thick and heavy and vulgarly expensive as possible. A few months later I again had occasion to interview him. When he was ten minutes late, I sent word to him with one of his entourage, "Tell the Vice-President if he keeps me waiting any longer, I'll return his bracelet." With his delightful humor he sent word back, "Tell her to send her arm along with it."

Hubert Humphrey had all the ingredients necessary to make a fine President. He is warm, compassionate, outgoing, brilliant, a controlled liberal. He is a pragmatist and supported those liberal causes which were in the realm of possibility. His Achilles' heel was his loyalty to Johnson. Why he had to conduct himself like a Boy Scout and swear allegiance to Johnson in his conduct of the war is beyond me. Had he come out opposing the continuation of the war, he could have defeated Mr. Nixon, whom I also interviewed. He has the charm that President Nixon does not have, but President Nixon, on the other hand, has tremendous personal discipline and has absorbed his former defeats and humiliations and turned them into extraordinary strength and perspicacity. He is an amazing man. It is unreasonable to expect lightheartedness and a fear of public disapproval from a man who has faced formidable defeats. Few men have enjoyed the triumph Mr. Nixon enjoyed in November 1972 but indubitably his triumph has been tainted and extinguished by Watergate.

But fate was kind. It gave Nixon Senator McGovern, who was doomed by his own nature, by bad luck, and by too many eccentric followers. An unspoken, a hidden, a furtive racism was registered against McGovern and brought many votes to Nixon.

When Sargent Shriver was selected as the vice-presidential candidate, I hurried to arrange an interview because, given the previous candidate's rapid rise and fall, I had no way of knowing how long he would remain the candidate. The interview was arranged for ten o'clock Saturday morning. I enjoined his advance man to see to it that Mr. Shriver was on time, for we had an extra crew standing by (overtime) and I had an engagement at eleven o'clock. The secret servicemen examined the premises (the deaths of John and Robert Kennedy have resulted in great precautions to safeguard the life of the President, the Vice-President, and candidates for the presidency.) They looked me over carefully; but, undoubtedly, concluded that I wasn't much of a hazard. But they didn't know about my temper. It was twenty-nine minutes after ten o'clock before Mr. Shriver appeared. He was urbane, cheerful, and cordial, ignoring his half-hour tardiness; but I was neither cheerful nor unaware of his tardiness.

"So sorry, Miss Fuldheim, I had some important business."

I knew full well it wasn't important business but dallying over his breakfast and I said so.

"How do you know?" he asked.

I actually didn't, but I took a chance that was the real reason. So while he was dallying, I was fuming.

One other time that I know of Shriver was late, was at an affair given for George Meany. It was unforgivable because his tardiness was due to a tennis game he was engaged in. Mr. Meany looked upon it as a personal slight.

One time when I was in Paris there was a press conference and Shriver was late to that, but then we weren't as impatient as Mr. Meany. Whether this had anything to do with Mr. Meany's attitude during the campaign, I don't know. But we all pay for our sins of omission as well as commission.

In the course of the interview I mentioned the cost of food as the chief worry of most Americans. "Oh yes," he said, "I know about the cost of food. I frequently push a cart in the supermarket."

"Mr. Shriver," I retorted, "you are handsome, knowledgeable, urbane; but don't try to make me believe you know what it is like to be poor. You have to experience poverty to understand the problems, the fears, the inferiority, the hopelessness of the poor."

It is significant because in the future elected offices will belong to the rich, only the rich will be able to afford to run. Who will speak for the poor? On the other hand, a man as fabulously wealthy as Governor Rockefeller is not likely to get himself in the position Vice-President Spiro Agnew did because money is not one of his worries, nor would he ever be involved in borrowing money to buy land and a house as President Nixon did. I admired him enormously for marrying the woman he loved, though it undoubtedly deprived him of the Republican nomination for President. He told me that there were priorities in life and he willingly accepted them. He is a rational liberal and certainly equipped to handle the position of President with integrity.

When the late John Kennedy, as senator, was preparing the ground swell for his nomination by the Democratic party for the presidency, a friend of mine called me and said, "You know, I'm a Republican but a close friend of mine, who is a Democrat, has asked me to give a dinner for Senator Kennedy. I'd appreciate it if you would join us."

"Sure," I answered, "I don't mind going to a dinner paid for by a Republican [the legend is that all Republicans are rich] in honor of a Democratic senator who may some day be president." There were about forty guests and Senator Kennedy spoke informally. Afterward, my host asked me what I thought. With amazing political perspicacity I answered, "He will never make it." After Kennedy was elected my host told me that he wanted to invite Kennedy to be his house guest but his wife vetoed it. He said he never forgave her! House cleaning was going on, and she didn't want to add to the confusion.

No matter what the merits of John Kennedy as a President, the fact remains that for a brief while there was glamour, a recognition of the arts and sciences, and good taste at the White House. The Kennedys created a legend, to do so in so few years was no mean achievement.

Of all the candidates that I have met, I enjoyed Harry Truman the most. He could have been described as an average American who rose to the exigencies of his position as President with incomparable courage and a high sense of the exalted responsibility of his office. He was no romantic figure, he was no Adlai Stevenson with a gift of oratory, but he was a man of character, sensibility, and good sense. I interviewed him in his Washington office just before FDR died and he became President. We had a long discussion about contemporary paintings. Later he was at the National Press Club where I was given an award for my interview with the first brainwashed prisoners released by the Chinese and again at a Democratic dinner in Cleveland where I paid him a tribute which, I'm told moved him.

He was gutsy, smart, generous; his character formed

by hard knocks; fiercely devoted to his daughter and wife. When confronted with high responsibility, he met it promptly and fearlessly.

The late FDR was not rich in the same sense as a Rockefeller, but he was accustomed to a life free of financial worries. It was an ironic twist of fate that this man, martyred by a cruel disease, should have faced the burden of a war so catastrophic and have handled himself as though he were not burdened by crutches and braces. Who will ever know the exhausting burden of standing with the weights on his legs? But his handicap never dwarfed or poisoned or perverted his outlook. It was under Franklin Delano Roosevelt that Social Security became a reality and in a great measure Social Security is responsible for saving us from an economic debacle. Of all measures passed, Social Security has offered us great economic stability and prevented millions from suffering abject poverty; it has guaranteed purchasing power to millions, which in turn assures employment for thousands. It is one of the noblest pieces of legislation ever passed in all man's history and it was passed during the administration of a man who was in physical pain a great part of the time.

Americans are unique. They are different from any other peoples. Every American carries in his bloodstream the heritage of the malcontent and the dreamer. Dukes didn't emigrate, only the dissatisfied—those who hungered for a life of freedom where they could believe, worship, and think with freedom. They dreamed a great dream that they and their children would be free of poverty. They dreamed of a life free of tyranny and the divine rights of kings. In their log cabins through the long winter nights these pioneers, as they gazed into the starry heavens, fashioned their dreams out of hope and strength.

The women bore their children alone and frequently

buried them alone. They came from all corners of the earth—France, Scotland, Germany, England, Italy—Protestant, Catholic, Jew. They intermingled. They became the first genuine United Nations in the history of mankind. The nineteenth century witnessed an unparalleled migration to North America animated by an intoxicating hope of a new concept of living.

They labored, these immigrants, and turned this continent into so powerful an engine of production, that today our G.N.P. is 30 per cent of the entire world's output. With each achievement their optimism, their gusto, their verve, grew into a national characteristic of generosity and strength—an assurance that all things were possible.

There never was anything like the vitality of these immigrants who became conquerors of a whole continent. Their dream of a good life became a reality. This intermingling of various nationalities produced a unique people. They came to this continent speaking a hundred different languages, their passion was to lose their differences, to be Americans, all speaking the same language. They developed their own mores and life style. They were building something new in the history of man and they rocked the world with amazement and envy.

Then there came a day when a woman arose and sang a mighty song:

Mine eyes have seen the glory of the coming of the Lord

· ·

As he died to make men holy, let us die to make men free.

A gethsemane of fire and anguish followed, but this remarkable people continued their march toward a new concept of freedom and unity. They were the first people to conceive of a nation without poverty.

They had done what had never been done before—created a nation made up of many peoples; created a nation out of a dream and with their brawn and muscle carved a continent. They were the modern Caesars, each wore a crown of victory. Theirs was a victory that marked each American with a toughness, a sureness, a roughness, an ability to perform, a simple sense of justice and a vitality that could conquer all.

Their dream of a better life had become a reality.

And each President in his own way carried this heritage in his genes and chromosomes and each had his own brand of bravery, gusto, and common sense. Deep in the heart of each one is the pioneer ancestor who came to the American shores following a star of promise for a better life.

Paris

In 1968 I was in Paris as the guest of the Japanese government. I wouldn't have spent a dollar of my own money, not while De Gaulle was in power. His unspent anger and frustration over the Americanization of France as well as of the rest of the world led him into Olympic errors. To endeavor to destroy the integrity of the American dollar by a gold run was not only stupid but the height of ingratitude, though it was covered up by high-minded words which meant nothing and which De Gaulle could use effectively. The American dollar is the only currency in the world which is redeemable by gold. The dollar was chosen by the world as the international money unit, and understandably so, for after the Second World War the United States was the one solvent nation of the great powers.

This America, this United States, performed a miracle unparalleled in all of history. An unbelievable performance! We fought a war in the Atlantic and the Pacific. We expanded the industrial complex to such a degree that we were able to provide our allies with armament. We equipped our own army for the European as well as the Japanese war. We sent troops across both oceans and we created a high degree of prosperity in our own country. And then Lend-Lease helped restore the economy of our allies. In addition, we did the unheard of—restored our enemies' economic life, that of Germany and Japan. Our performance during the war and the immediate years after was an awe-inspiring achievement.

We also maintained an army in Europe to prevent the Russian octopus from consuming more nations. We established NATO and we continued to pour millions and millions of dollars into Europe's devastated industry and economy. Eisenhower even delayed the taking of Paris so that De Gaulle could march at the head of the Allied troops. France was a conquered country freed by the Allies. Yet it was France that threw out NATO but did not hesitate to continue taking American dollars. It was De Gaulle who started the run on the American dollar. Had he succeeded, the monetary systems of the world would have been in complete chaos. Why did this man, capable of turning stubbornness into greatness, become so anti-American? His distaste for the invasion of Americanisms, he said, which corrupted the purity of the French language, imposed American drugstores, American efficiency, American supermarkets, and American technical know-how on France and the rest of the world. American pre-eminence in the world filled him with resentment and he truly believed that he could restore French greatness just by asserting that France was great. He did give France one moment of splendor and greatness when he withdrew the French Army from Algeria.

French greatness lies in its unique culture, which has influenced the world. If there had been no France, the world would be less beautiful and exciting. But technical efficiency, no! Try and get a new phone installed in Paris. Two years is not an unusual wait. One million tourists rush to Paris every year to behold the ugliest of all structures, the Eiffel Tower. Yet in fifty years, no new hotel was built in Paris until Hilton built one some years ago. You need never be lonely. Wherever I've wandered I've encountered a Hilton Hotel—Tel Aviv, Istanbul, Hawaii, Hong Kong, Berlin; they cover the earth.

So I was billeted by the Japanese at the Hilton in Paris and like all Hiltons the rooms were cheerful and spotless. Since it was an American hotel it boasted a coffee shop, a dining arrangement that I have always thought completely uncivilized and lacking in good taste, good food, and comfort, for the tables are so close together that it is impossible to avoid hearing the conversation of the guests at the tables next to yours. In my own case, being a gossip and an interested eavesdropper, I can't concentrate on my own thoughts; I do listen to the conversations at near-by tables.

One afternoon I dropped in for a cup of tea. After I had given my order the woman at the table next to mine smiled rather timidly at me and I returned the smile with a nod and a *"Bonjour."* Whereupon she leaned over and said, "You are an American."

How they can tell I don't know. I use French perfume but they always identify me as an American. I admitted that I was and we started a desultory conversation. I suggested that she join me, which she did with only a slight hesitation. I observed that she undoubtedly was a woman of limited means for she was wearing a jacket that did not match the skirt, a wool scarf that had been around a long time, and a hat which also had seen quite a number of winters. She was wearing a narrow gold wedding band and a ring which obviously was an engagement ring with a very tiny diamond. Personally I prefer the Liz Taylor type, bigger and more vulgar than anyone else's.

She explained in the course of our conversation that whenever she could afford it she came to the Hilton where she would see Americans and perhaps talk to some as she was to me.

"Why?" I inquired.

She was quite honest in her answer. "Well, it gives me a chance to use my English and besides I want to assure Americans that we are not all like De Gaulle, that many of us are indignant at what he says and does to Americans. Many of us entertain the liveliest sense of gratitude to America and we will never forget what Americans did for us."

I picked up the check. She had ordered only tea and toast and, observing her clothes, it was simple enough to conclude that she was living on a very small amount of money, perhaps a pension. But her pride was great. Because I had picked up the check she invited me to her apartment.

"I can't offer you much," she said, "but we could have a cup of coffee together."

I accepted with alacrity. I was grateful for the invitation for I have long ago given up the idea that I can get a significant story from the leaders of the world and I've interviewed a goodly number, from Hitler to Ben Gurion, from the late, infamous McCarthy to Kennedy, from the Shah of Iran to Truman to Wendell Willkie. But let me talk to the people—taxi drivers, hotel clerks, maids, storekeepers—and I will discover what they feel about their world, their leaders, the young, the United States, and what their dreams are. Very often I will sit on a bench in a park and sooner or later someone will join me. If I can speak the language, I will find out about their hopes and their frustrations. I have discovered that most people dream of a life such as the average American enjoys. This was before crime and drugs poisoned our lives. Their dreams do not always include the United States of today.

Mrs. French lived on the Left Bank near Republic Boulevard in a small apartment. She welcomed me with pleasure and immediately set about preparing the coffee. A small table was set up near the window with cups and silver and sweets. Separated from the living room by a velvet curtain, rather shabby through long service, was a small alcove where apparently there was a hot plate on which my French friend was heating the water for the coffee.

Wandering around the room I stopped in front of the fireplace over which there was a traditional marble mantelpiece. I observed that at one end there was a framed photograph of a man about fifty years old in uniform.

To make conversation I called out, "Madame, who is that gentleman?" What ensued then I shall remember through all the days of my life.

"That, madame," she answered, "was my father, who was killed in the First World War."

I glanced at the other end of the mantelpiece and I observed that at this end there also a photograph of a man in uniform, but younger, perhaps thirty-eight or forty years old.

"And who," I asked, "is that?"

"That," she replied, "is a photograph of my husband, who was killed in the Second World War."

I was distressed and in order to change the subject I pointed to an unframed photograph of a young man about nineteen or twenty years of age who was not in uniform and which occupied the center of the mantelpiece.

Thinking it was a safe question, I inquired, "And who is this young man?"

There was a silence for about thirty seconds until I turned, perplexed at her silence, about to repeat my question. I can still see her standing there, holding in her hand the kettle in which she was brewing the coffee.

Then she lifted the photograph in her hand, gazed at it for a few seconds, and answered, "That was my son Alfredo, who was killed in the war in Algeria."

Only the pen of a Greek dramatist can find words adequate to describe the agonized heart of a simple Frenchwoman who represents the torture and tragedy of this century. The stench of death surrounds the last sixty years. What shall we say of a century that defies time and space and ventures into the heavens, walking on the moon; which dreams of circumventing the speed of light; a century that produces an Einstein and a Hitler? What shall men do? Rend their garments in mourning? What lament is adequate for fifty million gory deaths as the result of war? Fifty million is beyond my ability to comprehend but to stand in a living room and hear this Frenchwoman describe her desolation, her tree of life stripped of all its leaves, was too much for me.

I wept, for I thought of how many doors had heard the rustle of the wings of the Angel of Death and how many young sleep their eternal sleep in darkness, denied the feel of the sun on their faces, the smell of lilacs in spring, the rapture of young love, and the wisdom of age. And for a moloch known as war. War which makes a mockery of achievements and puts us down very low on the ladder of evolution.

So I wept and a Frenchwoman who had known grief beyond description tried to comfort me.

A September
Afternoon

I interviewed Jeanne Dixon just after the dramatic story of her prognostication that John Kennedy would be assassinated. She told me that she saw two bags of gold on my shoulder. I was enormously interested. Money is such a nice thing to have. The dame who uttered the now famous and immortal words that diamonds are a girl's best friend certainly knew what she was talking about. "Are they little or big bags?" I asked. For the record, there have been neither little or big bags on my shoulders.

I am dubious about the ability of any human to see the future. If anyone can foresee future events, it would mean that everything is predestined; and it's pretty difficult to believe that it was destined that the furniture in my bedroom would be so arranged that I would stumble over the telephone cord and wrench my ankle. It may be that not a sparrow shall fall without God's knowing, but that must be poetic license, though it is possible to conceive that the essence of divinity is seeing and knowing all things that occur in the universe in each second at the same time.

I am skeptical about astrology. Astrologers assure me

with great certitude that the position of the stars and moon at my birth reveals events in my future. I have argued with my friend, Catherine DeJersey, a well-known astrologer, that astrology is not an exact science and the rules laid down by astrologers are not based on empirical evidence. What was good enough for the ancient Egyptians is not enough for an expanding universe. But no matter, it fills space in newspapers and is elegantly featured in *Vogue*. And it ill becomes me to be cynical; I have my own superstitions—I always knock on wood, but I am having a bad time because so many things are now made of plastic, and plastic will not do to keep away disaster—it must be wood, so I'm thinking of carrying a piece of wood in my purse.

The stars may not regulate our lives, but we are prisoners of our chromosomes and genes. Even before birth the pattern of our physical as well as psychic life is outlined. Admitting that environment has a good deal to do with the way we develop, yet two people in exactly the same set of circumstances will react in totally different ways.

We are imprisoned by our genetic code. Given a certain kind of person there is an inevitability about what his conduct will be. Some are destined for tragedy; others, for a pedestrian life. Napoleon was a gambler. He gambled with thousands of lives and he repeated it over and over. In everything he did Lincoln walked unerringly to his ultimate destiny. Read the story of Cleopatra's brief life and it is obvious that in the end her gambles always betrayed her. The last Nicholas of Russia was doomed because his intellect was limited, unequal to the thundering demands of a new century.

The pattern of our lives is not written in the stars, but in our genes. The passionate, the intense, never take life lightly for if they can love deeply and wildly, they are capable of other wildness. I remember once a number of years ago sitting in the Bois in Paris with a friend and discussing the power of temperament and how it rules our lives. At that moment, we saw two women approaching a bench near by. My friend exclaimed, "How providential. I know the older woman and her life exemplifies your theory that we do what our heritage compels us to do. The woman is Madame Chatelet. Let me tell you her story."

Madame Chatelet walked with her cane to give her legs some support. Her neighbor guided her to a bench.

"Now, Madame, if you will sit here I will be back for you in less than an hour. I must do my shopping for the weekend. Don't try to walk without me; it wouldn't be comfortable to fall and injure your back."

"I know, I know," sighed Madame Chatelet. "In another few months I will be eighty-six years."

"What kind of pessimistic talk is that! What you should say is that in fourteen years you will be one hundred years old."

Madame Chatelet smiled. "I am grateful to you. You are a wonderful neighbor. Without you I couldn't get out of the apartment. But don't hurry. Just finish your shopping. I'll be quite comfortable here on the bench."

It was a golden September afternoon. A week of incessant rain had washed the skies into a true heavenly blue. The leaves of the trees were a shining green as though they had been polished, the grass was clean. No wind was blowing and the flower gardens in the distance looked as though they were painted on the ground.

People strolling by would sometimes nod or smile as they passed. Madame had a sweet face and was very tiny, resembling a Dresden doll that had aged. Sometimes when she looked at her face in the mirror, which she rarely did except to see if her hair was parted evenly, she was faintly surprised at how different she looked from her mental image of herself. There were many photographs of herself taken when she was young and it was this image she had of herself. This old face with its lines around the eyes and the shriveled neck, this was a disguise that she was wearing temporarily and it slightly nauseated her. Her hands, once so white and smooth, had been compared to a swan's breast. Nowadays she found herself clenching them to straighten out the wrinkles. But it was an effort and she had to smile at her own vanities.

A few leaves fell on her shoulders. She brushed them off. She noticed that not far from where she was sitting there was a flower stand piled high with nasturtiums, brilliant and gay flowers of orange and yellow and a touch of red. Why did the sight of the nasturtiums cause a violent emotion to sweep over her? Then she remembered. They were the first flowers that Pierre had sent her; she recalled opening the box to find a corsage of nasturtiums with purple ribbons and the card reading, "Because these colors remind me of you."

"Did this happen to me," she thought, "and how long ago was it? Sixty years ago?" Was she in her twenties then? Yes, it must have been. She had almost forgotten his name for a moment. Why did she burn so for him? What was there about him that held her enthralled? How many nights she had slipped from the house, when she was not performing, while the child was sleeping, to meet him halfway as he walked through the park from his office. Why could she not recapture the ecstasy and excitement of being with him? It had changed her life—ruined it, she thought wryly, would be a better word—and now she could not recapture the memory of her passion. For him she had left her husband. Where was the glory that had burned her with such ecstasy? She tried to remember what he looked like. He had black hair, thick and wavy. In his arms she would stroke the waves and kiss the top of his head. She was frail in those days, too. He would lift her up and carry her as though she were a child. He would croon, "My sweet, my love, my baby. I will love you forever."

"That's not enough. It must be forever and ever."

"Forever. Even after death."

Her husband called her a loose woman, a whore, unfit to be the mother of their child. She did not dare sue for divorce. The court would have awarded the child to her husband.

"Why," demanded Pierre, "did you ever marry him?"

"How can I describe the reasons and are they important?" she asked. "I do not love him, it is you whom I love. How was I to know when I married him that there was such love and passion that I feel for you. You are a storm of fire, a rapture for me. I love you, Pierre, very much. Isn't that enough?"

He held her close. "I am satisfied, my darling."

He was at every performance. He had a box reserved and soon all of Paris knew of "the affair" as it was described. He was wealthy and she was lovely to look at, and had the added mystique of being a popular actress.

The sight of the brilliant colored flowers set off a host of memories in her mind. She was trying to remember exactly what happened, what changed. She began to notice a change in his devotion. His ardor was diminishing and he began to have business engagements. His seat at the theater was empty. She was proud, but her love was greater than her pride. She had phoned only to be told that he was not at home. Gossip columnists began to hint about a rift between Madame Chatelet and M. Rothschild. The telephone remained a mute instrument. What was it? Why didn't he call? Anything was better than not knowing.

"I'm no woman of the street to be treated this way," she thought.

What could she do? Anger at his neglect and yearning for his presence alternated in her feelings. The hunger to see him, and to know what had happened, at last drove her to his apartment in spite of her pride, and, astonishingly enough, he was at home. She was trembling as she confronted him. Did he no longer love her?

"Oh no, darling, it's just that I've been busy. Nothing is wrong."

"Busy for two weeks?"

"But you see, I was in Bordeaux and in London on the firm's business."

"Aren't there any telephone lines between Paris and London?" Her voice quivered and she could not contain her tears. "I do not believe you," she said accusingly.

"Oh, come, baby, no tears, sit here with me."

It was easier to take his excuses, it was easier to be lulled into accepting his explanation. The comfort of his arms around her was a sanctuary.

"I love your perfume. It fits you perfectly. No more tears, though, I must say, you are beautiful even when you are crying."

Two hours of love-making and her world was restored for her. Nevertheless, a few nights later, his seat was again empty and there were no telephone calls. Now she was sure she had been betrayed. Columnists began gossiping about M. Rothschild's attentions to Mademoiselle Richardo. A month later the engagement of M. Rothschild and Mademoiselle Richardo was announced.

What happened to her then? Why was she so distraught? She was trying to recall the violent emotion, the insanity that led her to try to kill him. She was unable to remember what led her to take the gun and drive to Pierre's office.

She remembered that there was something in her brain that exploded at the time she pulled the trigger and shot him. He stood there and his coat sleeve slowly stained itself with blood. And then he slumped to the floor. She knew she returned to her apartment, though she had no memory of returning home, because that's where the police found her.

It was the sensation of Paris but Pierre did not die, though he had an arm that hung limply by his side for the rest of his life.

She refused to plead innocent and the court found her guilty. The newspapers wrote of this woman who had everything—beauty, talent, a husband and a child. What would lead her to try and commit murder? She never defended herself and she spent seven years in jail. Seven Christmases, seven Easters, seven Bastille Days, seven years, seven springs, seven summers, seven falls and seven winters. How did she endure them? Seven years of silence, for she rarely spoke. The jailers were more gentle with her than with most of the prisoners. She refused to see anyone. She would talk to no one. The endless days, like a procession of gray hours, stretched out, it seemed to her, forever. One day and a night passed by. The next day and night stood by waiting to take over. The prison clothes were the worst. Her delicate skin chaffed against the rough and what seemed to her brutal material. She read and reread whatever was available. An anonymous friend sent her a collection of fish. The warden allowed her to keep them. They became her friends; like the fish she, too, was a prisoner, fed and kept warm and alive so that the gray and endless days could imprison her. Her cell was changed so that she looked out on a tree and in the summer an occasional bird or butterfly would flutter the leaves. How wonderful to be a bird and to be free. At first she prayed voicelessly, "Let me die, God, let me die."

There were no pills to take, so only prayers were left
and God did not answer. He had other plans for her. When
at the end of seven years she was told that in a month she
would be free, she was terrified. Where would she go?
What would she do? Her lawyer came to meet her and
took her away in a cab to his own apartment. His wife
welcomed her and with the small amount of money she had
in the bank she was able to rent a modest apartment.

The world was a wonderful place. Just to walk down
the streets was exhilarating. She bathed three times a day
to feel the luxury of a warm, perfumed bath. It was weeks
before she could rid herself of the memory of the odor of
the jail. She took many baths with perfume and cream and
oils before her skin felt clean.

Every day she walked out into the street to hear the
sound of cars and voices, to watch people going and coming freely. Every day she bought a few flowers to smell,
a sweet clean odor. She bought bottles of perfume and
poured the perfume on her sheets and blankets. She could
not get enough of fresh and sweet smells. Things she had
never noticed before enchanted her, like the lace curtains
swaying as the wind moved them, China cups, not mugs, to
hold as she drank her coffee. To walk into a store and buy
a dress, to see merchandise—an endless variety—not to
have to march to a table and eat only on orders, to sleep
on linen sheets again. It was like an enchantment.

But she also knew that in a few months she would have
to earn a living. Her money would be gone. What could
she do? Her only talent was acting and who would hire
her, a released prisoner? Certainly not in Paris. Maybe in
the provinces. She would have to try.

It was difficult. She changed her name and was given a
few parts, just enough roles to survive. She was still lovely
to look at but the fire was gone. She could no longer feel

much. One of the directors in exasperation told her the
fact that she couldn't feel was no reason for not being able
to simulate emotions on stage and that if she couldn't
there would be no more roles for her. Her career as an
actress was over. She was washed up. She remembered trying for one job after another until finally she was engaged
as housemother in one of the private schools for young
boys.

She was, she recalled, forty years of age when she first
went there. The years went by and then she was fifty-three
and then she was sixty-three and suddenly she knew she was
old. The gold of her hair was all gone. What had been
ethereal loveliness now was just being thin and frail. The
boys had been fond of her and she had been grateful for
the quiet and unobtrusive life she led. Her daughter had
married an American and wrote her infrequently and her
husband had divorced her long ago while she was still in
jail. She had few friends and she avoided anyone she had
known before the shooting of Pierre.

In the school there was one little chap, seven years old,
to whom she was very drawn. Perhaps it was because he
was small for his age and was ragged and teased by the
larger boys. In a tussle he received a bloody nose and she
had kept him against regulations in her room all night.
When he left for the summer vacation he actually clung to
her and she found herself looking forward to his return.
He told her all about his two older brothers, who were a
pain in the neck, and his sister, who was a real creep, and
his father, whom he adored, and his grandfather, who was
terrible.

When he was thirteen years old he was sent to school in
London. She missed him and every so often he would send
her a card and she would carefully send him one in return.

When she was sixty-five years old she was obliged to retire. Her pension was very meager. It meant living in one room with just barely enough francs a month to survive. And she was lonely for she had made few friends. It was a bleak outlook but when she remembered her years in prison she did not rebel.

Some years after her retirement she received a letter from a Parisian firm of solicitors. They had been instructed to see to it that every three months she was to receive a check for fifteen hundred francs and that their client wished to remain unknown. Would she inform them where she would be residing?

The letter fluttered from her hands. Who was it that was sending her the money? She was baffled and thought perhaps there was a mistake, but she was assured there was no mistake. She was Madame Chatelet, was she not?

That was over ten years ago. Now she was old and having difficulty recalling the strange events of her life. She was lonely, too. She was like one of those burnt out stars that astronomers describe that flash for a few years and then are gone forever. How many more days would she sit on a bench and watch the living, for already she was no longer living, only waiting. It was like the days in the jail, waiting for an end. Suddenly she remembered a night in Pierre's arms when he had held her from him and said, "You look like a shining star." How of all her memories did this one come back to her? Where was he now? Was he still living or, like herself, only waiting, knowing his bank account of living days would soon be used up.

She shivered and drew her wrap around herself. Now she noticed a young couple coming toward her. The young man was carrying some flowers. He stopped in front of her.

"Madame," he said, "I thought you might enjoy these fresh nasturtiums. We noticed you sitting here alone." And he placed the bouquet with its purple ribbons on her lap and raised her hands to his lips. The girl with him smiled and said, "*Bonjour*, Madame."

As they walked away she asked, "What made you give them to her? I thought you bought the flowers for me."

"Because she is the woman who shot my grandfather and he deserved it. He was really a bastard. As soon as I came into my inheritance I provided for her. She doesn't know it nor did she recognize me as the young kid who went to Lavonne Academy, where she was a housemother, to whom she was very kind."

Madame Chatelet held the brilliant flowers in her hand, which was shaking, and raised them to her face. How kind people really were. Maybe when she died God would be kind to her.

"Quite a story," I said. "Do you think anything could have saved her from her destiny?" I asked.

My friend shrugged her shoulders. "I don't know. I'm familiar with her story because I'm one of the solicitors who arranged that young Rothschild's request of the gift of francs be sent to her anonymously every quarter. He was a student in the school where she worked as house-mother. She was kind to him and when he came into his inheritance, he arranged for an allowance for her."

Television Sucks
a Performer Dry

Television is a grueling business. It consumes all one's talent and inner resources, it literally sucks one dry. Before radio and television, a performer could use the same material a thousand times and not cover the entire country. One performance on television and millions see the act, necessitating new material. In addition, it's nerve-racking, and the discipline necessary to prepare a cool and tranquil appearance on the air is enormous. Few people have any idea of the strain. After twenty-seven years I still feel apprehension at certain times, such as when I am handling a delicate problem like the Kent episode or a labor dispute or an important interview such as with President Nixon or John Connally. Appearing every day with new material inevitably means that some shows are bound to be dull. I hold post-mortems after many commentaries and torture myself as to why I didn't handle the subject more adroitly or more interestingly, like cardplayers who go over the hands they held.

Then there are the struggles to get a decent picture on TV. One day I had just finished a tape and asked the director to run it for me as I wasn't sure of one of my statements. I was shocked when I saw the picture.

"I have a black beard on my chin. Where did it come from?" I demanded.

"What black beard?" asked the floorman. "I don't see any."

"Are you blind?"

He turned to another floorman: "Do you see any beard?"

"Not exactly. I do see a small shadow under your chin, but it's hardly visible."

I'm exasperated. I summon the lightman. "Why have I got a beard?"

He shrugs his shoulders. "I don't know; the lighting is the same as always."

"It can't be. I've never had a beard before." Silence greets this statement.

Then, "You are wearing a white collar and that causes a shadow."

"I've worn white collars before, and there's been no beard. How come there is one today?"

"Everyone has a shadow under their chin."

I'm ready to explode. "I watched *Maude* last night, and she didn't have a beard."

Silence on the floor, all the floormen looking bored.

"Get the light supervisor, and let him look at the picture," I demanded.

The supervisor arrives and actually examines the film. "Yes, the shadow is too great. We will change the lighting."

I'm vindicated, but too exasperated to do the show over. And unbeknownst to me, a free-lance writer for the *Clevelander* magazine is in the studio preparing to do a story on me. When the story was published, it started with "The Bearded Lady." I groaned, and then remembered what

Harry Truman advised, "If you can't take the heat, stay out of the kitchen."

Then, there is the teleprompter. Every so often it breaks down in the middle of a broadcast and whenever it does this, it's always during my commentary, never during that of the other news personnel. I'm sure it's bewitched—under a spell. It's maddening to lose your copy in the middle of a sentence; this happened to me one evening. Fortunately, I was able to go on. I picked it up and went through the commentary without any hesitation because once I write a commentary it becomes fixed in my mind. When I finished, the news team applauded me. It was almost worth the agony to receive their rare approval.

As far as we know, I'm the only woman in the country who has had her own news show in a major market. I did a fifteen-minute news show at six-thirty every evening with the same sponsor, Duquesne beer, for seventeen years. The officers of the company and Victor Maitland, a vigorous, original, and very effective advertising man at that time, were wonderful to me. It was a relationship that was very unusual. At first they knew nothing about me and bought me only because they wanted the time segment, figuring they would get rid of me in thirteen weeks, but keep the time. The relationship lasted for over seventeen years until there was a reorganization of the company.

Being a woman has its advantages. I can say things no man can. On the other hand, in the past I've been treated patronizingly because I am a woman. That always bores me. Remove the brain from a body and there's no way of telling whether it is a male or female brain. What really enrages me is to be told that I think "like a man." Of course this attitude is changing more and more; women are breaking into all fields. Nevertheless, television and radio are dominated by the male. It's a masculine and youth-oriented business.

Why men are especially adapted for news reporting is difficult to understand. There are some female reporters in TV newsrooms—generally one. This is to prove that the station has no prejudices. They may have no prejudices but the fact remains that women are few and far between in television. I'm the rare exception.

The impact of television in our lives is incredible. How fully the medium has taken over was demonstrated to me one evening last September. WEWS is on the corner of East Thirtieth and Euclid in Cleveland where there is a bus stop. I was standing outside waiting for my car when the bus stopped. A frail, small woman in her sixties emerged from the bus and stopped and stared at me. She was, apparently, a woman of modest means. Her cotton skirt had been washed so often the pattern was faded and colorless.

"Is it really you?" she asked. I admitted the fact, and we started to talk.

"You've been visiting?" I asked.

"Yes," she answered. "I go to see my daughter every Thursday and I can afford the bus fare because she always gives me my dinner for the next day," as she held up a paper bag.

"Where do you live?" I asked.

"In the high-rise down Thirtieth Street," she answered, "which is about four blocks down."

"Do you work?" I asked.

"Oh, no. You see my hands are arthritic," and she stretched them out for me to observe.

"What do you live on? Do you have a pension?"

"No, but I have Social Security, so you see I'm all right." All the time she was examining me with great curiosity.

"My, my," she said. "I never thought I'd really see you in person. You look just like you do on television. Wait till I tell my friends."

I was interested in her. She was friendly and, apparently, awed at meeting someone in television. She was a frail, little woman shorter than I, which is something. If I ever live again in some reincarnate form, I'm going to have the longest legs any woman has ever had. Have you ever noticed how most men look at a woman? From the feet up! Well, the viewing of my legs is short, very short!

"Do you have a family?"

"Just a daughter. I have no one else."

"Do you mind telling me what your Social Security benefits are?"

"No, I don't mind. It's seventy-six dollars and forty cents a month."

"What is your rent?"

"Thirty-seven dollars and fifty cents," she replied.

"Can you manage on your Social Security?"

"I am all right. I manage and I'm not lonely because, you see, I have two friends."

"Who are they?" I inquired.

And with great honesty, though a littly shyly, she told me, "God and my television."

This shook me, and it was then I realized how great a role television plays in our lives and how great the responsibility to maintain good taste and high standards of speech. The impact and influence of television is far greater than the movies ever were.

There can be no doubt that we are a better informed and educated people because of television. Soap operas may not be productive of more knowledge, more erudition, but who can say how many lonely hours have been filled because of them? There have been great dramas presented on television, affording millions to see incredibly moving theater, and beautiful ballets, scientific information, operas, all have been made available on TV.

And who will ever forget the night television showed

the first human being to walk on the moon? This must surely have been television's greatest hour.

We may not all be invited to a royal wedding, but we were actually present at Princess Margaret's and Princess Anne's. How many hearts beat with sorrow to the sound of Jackie Kennedy's footsteps as she followed the hearse carrying her assassinated husband, the President of the United States? Who will ever forget the moment of intense drama when Jack Ruby shot Lee Harvey Oswald with at least half the nation watching? And Watergate, when a nation watched history being enacted?

Television has given me the opportunity to know and become acquainted with people from all walks of life.

My friends are legion and I'm particularly fond of taxi drivers. I use them so often that when any one of them sees me walking, they pull up to the curb to greet me. In a big city where one can be very lonely, this is a wonderful, cheering thing.

The other day when I got into a cab, the wind had blown my hair so that I looked disheveled. I had no comb; the driver looked at me disapprovingly, pulled out his comb, wiped it on his sleeve, handed it to me with, "Here, use mine, you look awful." That's friendship!

Then there was the female taxi driver who said as I emerged from the cab in front of the TV station, "Baby, you're something!" Well, that interested me; I can't resist any approval.

"Why am I something?"

"Well, my old man always says to me, 'Why ain't you as smart as Dorothy?'" (Everyone calls me "Dorothy.")

"What do you say to him?" I asked her.

"Oh," she answered, "I sez, if you are so smart, why ain't you the President of the United States?"

The telephones ring, and the mail comes pouring in whenever I report on guns. All the gun lovers bombard me with the usual arguments as to why there should be no laws against the possession of guns. All their arguments leave me cold. All I know is that there are thousands of deaths caused by guns every year.

When I interviewed Jane Fonda, the anti-war proponents cheered and the hard hats violently disapproved by mail and by phone. During Lt. Calley's trial the calls were bitter. The possibility of an increase in Social Security benefits brings in hundreds of frantic calls asking when will the increase begin. Ten dollars more is vastly important to a man living on a hundred and eighty dollars a month.

Then there are other calls. "I've listened to you for years but after tonight I'm through with you." This was particularly true during the Watergate hearings. It takes a disciplined person to listen to convictions which are different from their own. I've had good training in that. I read William Buckley and he can frequently be irritating. The night I interviewed him, he came into the studio needing a shoeshine and a haircut.

"Ah," I said, "Louis XIV himself."

He grinned and retorted, "I hear you deliver some mighty blows yourself, and I'm prepared." He made an engaging guest because he is brilliant and has a magnificent command of English.

Then there are the calls from people who are in distress: they can't find an apartment that they can afford; their welfare check hasn't arrived; the man next door has an air-conditioning unit that makes so much noise, they can't sleep; what do you think of psychiatrists; why is the Senate wasting time on Watergate; what is this country coming to; why doesn't the President do something about the price of calves' liver—$2.48 a pound? Why won't Blue Cross pay for chemotherapy?

It is, indeed, true that most people lead lives of quiet desperation. They have problems, and no one to turn to.

If they call their councilman, he gives them the runaround; if they write their congressmen, they receive a form letter; their senators are unapproachable and they hang up the phone dejected and rejected by life.

They call me because after so many years, they look upon me as their friend, and I'm not likely to deny them the right of friendship. They feel better after they've told me their woes.

In my commentaries, as in my lectures, I avoid the generalizations. I use the specific. It's great to be Olympic and talk about credit, devaluation, etc. It is far more persuasive to illustrate in simple figures how much more you will pay on your mortgage each month if the interest rate goes up from 5 per cent to 9½ per cent. One doesn't have to have a Ph.D. in economics to understand that.

To report that fifty-five thousand American boys were killed in the war does not bring tears, that is remote and an impersonal statistic, but describe one household with a bedroom that will never be occupied by the son, a guitar that will never be played again, a baby that will never hear the sound of his father's voice, and you have made your point about the cost of wars.

To be able to humanize the news is the ideal and the newscaster who can do that is bound to be successful, for there are few who respond to abstract postulations and impersonal accounts compared to those who respond to almost everything emotionally. It's ridiculous to hear an anchorman report a killing with exactly the same expression as if he were reporting a recipe to make applesauce. News reported in newspapers must of necessity be impersonal. But a broadcaster is a human being and should cease acting like a feelingless printing press pouring out the news.

A great deal of criticism has been hurled at newsmen. They have been accused of lacking objectivity. That's a lot of hogwash! If a newsman reports on Mr. Mitchell's testimony before the Senate, he reports what Mitchell's responses were and certainly his most important statements. Newsmen are brave and have courage. Covering wars means facing death and capture by the enemy, as occurred in Vietnam. The disdain expressed by some of the men in Washington for the press was entirely unjustified. While they remained safely in Washington, the newsmen were facing incredible danger to bring back the story of the war. Ernie Pyle was only one of the many of those who died trying to do their job. Columnists and commentators' jobs are quite different; their function is to interpret what has occurred based on their knowledge and historic evaluations.

If it had not been for the great tradition of newsmen and their ability to ferret out and trace down stories, the American people would never have known about Watergate and all of the bizarre and dishonest maneuvering in order to win an election. Deceit, dishonesty, lying, spying, blackmailing, all were used, and those who surrounded Mr. Nixon apparently believed that anything and everything was permissible just so it ensured Mr. Nixon's re-election. Though it has always seemed to me that those who directed President Nixon's campaign for re-election couldn't have been very astute. Practically any dumbbell could have figured out that any Republican could have defeated Senator McGovern. It wasn't necessary to spend sixty million dollars on the campaign.

News people are the vigilantes. They should be encouraged, not penalized. It is with their help that freedom is retained and maintained in the United States. Abort or infringe on freedom of the press, and we are on the ladder leading to fascism.

$3,400

What are coincidences? Are they purely fortuitous or does destiny balance each event with a pattern which we do not always perceive. Destiny is sometimes thwarted but always wins in the end. For every white light there must be black darkness, a darkness which comes to demand payment no matter how long delayed. Is the judgment seat only a mythological anthropomorphic concept of the eternal law that all of us pay somewhere along our path? For every rapture there is a price and nothing is sustained forever. The path that destiny takes in the end leads to a balance of payments. No one remains overdrawn forever. Destiny's bank is inexorable, all accounts must balance.

I reflected on this after I left the home of a friend of mine whose name is Lenore Strafferd. She is a beautiful woman with exquisite skin, olive-hued with a touch of rose, and eyes literally as black as coals. A figure with a tiny waist; a full, high bust; tall and willowy; an erect and graceful carriage. Botticelli would have yearned to paint her. She had literally led a charmed life, with a devoted husband and three sons that would have been anyone's

pride. When she was fifty, she was in an automobile accident and sustained a fractured leg and hip. There was no
assurance that she would ever walk without a cane or
crutch. This was a worry to her because she played tennis
and golf. Not only that, but she was active, never sat still,
was always up and doing something. She could sew. She
could paint. She worked with the blind. She entertained.
Her days and nights were full.

The day I went to see her she was in a wheel chair out
in the garden. It was a day so perfect that it must have
been the kind which Lowell described as, "And what is so
rare as a day in June? Then, if ever, come perfect days."
The smell of the first roses of June was in the air but my
friend looked pale and wan.

"My dear, my dear," I said. "What can I say? You know
how distressed I am."

She smiled. "Well, just say a prayer for me that I will
be able to walk again. You know, for fifty years I've used
my legs, my spine, my hip bones to walk and never thought
about the complicated joints and muscles needed to enable
me to walk. Only now am I aware of how clever nature
is. Besides," she said with a smile, "I have plenty of time to
think. My universe of thought and interests may be large
but my area of activities now is pretty limited."

At the moment her nurse appeared, a rather plain-look-
ing black woman about thirty-five years old.

"I'd better wheel you out of the sun."

"Yes, do," said my friend, "the sun on the water blinds
my eyes."

The nurse arranged the wheel chair so that Lenore
could look out at the lake that was shimmering and gleam-
ing with the radiance of the June day.

"She handles you gently, doesn't she?" I said.

"Yes," answered Lenore, as she gazed at the nurse who

was disappearing in the house. "You know, there is a strange relationship between us."

I looked startled. "What do you mean? What kind of relationship except that between nurse and patient?"

"Oh, she isn't aware of anything unusual in our relationship, but I am."

"What's the story?"

"Let me tell you. It only proves that truth is stranger than fiction. One day I asked her—by the way, her name is Ms. Stronge—'How did you happen to become a nurse? Did you always want to be one as a young girl?'

"'Yes,' she answered, 'ever since I was about ten years old I wanted to be a nurse because I saw a movie with a nurse as the leading character and I always dreamed of growing up and wearing the white cap and nurse's uniform. I used to daydream about working with the doctors and answering the summonses of the patients.'

"'I finished high school with an average of B+ and my mother and dad were proud. I was the only black girl who was going on to become a nurse. My dad was a porter in a commercial building. My mother worked in the kitchen of the YMCA. They didn't earn much but the combined salaries enabled them to buy a five-room house and since I was an only child, they managed.

"'I enrolled in a college for a pre-nursing course. At the end of the year my dad lost his job and couldn't find another one. For a while we managed on my mother's wages, but things got worse and her job was reduced from five days a week to two days. I decided I'd better give up the idea of becoming a registered nurse and take a practical nurse's course. But my dad was distressed. He was literally sick with disappointment. He was proud of being able to give me an education. I tried to console him. "Look, Dad, being a practical nurse isn't such a terrible thing and maybe some day when things get better, I can still go on training."

" 'He shook his head. "You don't understand. I never had an education but your mother and I made up our minds that you were not going to be a salad girl like your mother."

" ' "Why, Dad, what's wrong about being a salad girl?"

" ' "Nothing except we wanted better things for you."

" 'Well, a short time after, Mom had a heart attack. She couldn't work any more, so I got her job. My father was desperate. He still had no regular job. He did have a job in a parking lot on Thursday, Friday, and Saturday but he was depressed and with Mom sick and knowing I was giving up the hope of ever becoming a practical nurse, it was a sad household.

" 'I'd been working about two months when one morning my dad came to the YM and asked for me.

" ' "I want you to come home."

" ' "Why, is Mom worse?"

" ' "No, I just want you to come home. Tell the chef you're needed at home."

" 'I was frightened. I thought Mom had another attack, and he didn't want to tell me.

" ' "No, no," he assured me, "I want to show you something."

" ' "Couldn't it wait until I am through working? I may lose my job if I walk out."

" ' "No," he answered, "you're not going back to work, you're going back to school."

" 'I stared at him. Had his mind been affected?

" 'When we arrived home I said, "Now what's all this about? Why should I give up my job?"

" 'He didn't answer. Instead he opened a bureau drawer and pulled out a big Manila envelope. He handed it to me. I looked at it without touching it.

" ' "Open it. Go ahead. Just don't stand there."

" 'I opened it, bewildered, but my bewilderment was even greater when thirty-four hundred-dollar bills fell out. I stared.

" ' "Where did you get those?"

" ' "Well," he said, "you know I'm the last one out of the parking lot on Fridays. I was sweeping up when I saw this envelope. It looked dirty and soiled. I picked it up and sticking out about an inch was a hundred-dollar bill and there were thirty-four of them. I didn't tell you about it until I was sure I could keep it. I looked in the papers for a week in the lost columns. There was nothing in them to identify such a loss. That money is for you to finish your nursing course."

" ' "Gosh, Dad, shouldn't you go to the police and report finding the money?"

" ' "No, I'm not going to the police. This is for your education." '

"And that, she told me, was how she became a registered nurse. Her dad, very shortly afterwards got a regular job."

"But what has that story got to do with you?" I asked. "You said there is a relationship between you."

"Wait," answered my friend, "I haven't finished the story."

"Every year, she told me, her dad would take her to the spot where he found the money and say, 'I always want you to remember this is where our good fortune started.'

"She thought it was kind of silly to do this, but it pleased her dad so that she went along and always on that day he gives the church fifty dollars and so does she. It's kind of a good luck charm."

"Very interesting, but I still don't see what that's got to do with you except that you have an efficient nurse."

"Don't be so impatient. It's quite a story. I asked Ms. Stronge where her father found the envelope and what day it was and what year and where. She told me it was in Cleveland near the Central National Bank on June 26, 1955. And, you see, on that day I had gone to my safe-deposit box and had drawn thirty-four hundred dollars that I needed in a hurry. I put the money in one of the brown envelopes and put it on the back seat. I was in a hurry because I had a number of errands. I was leaving a suit, which was on the back seat, at the tailor. In my haste as I pulled the suit out, I must have pulled the envelope along with it and it fell out without my observing it. And not until I was halfway home did I become aware that the envelope was no longer in the seat. I drove back to the tailor and drove up and down the streets, but, of course, saw nothing."

"Why didn't you advertise in the lost column?"

"I was sure no one would answer because there was no identification on the envelope and I preferred not to have my husband know about the episode. I did go to the police, but they had no reports or record or clues.

"Well, the money her father found in Cleveland was on the same day around the area where I lost the envelope. It is not likely that two people would have lost thirty-four hundred dollars on the same day and in the same area that I did, so it must have been my money which he found."

Lenore shrugged her shoulders, "It wasn't a bad investment because now I have a fine nurse who I may need for a long time."

"God moves in mysterious ways, His wonders to perform," I murmured.

"Did you tell her?" I asked.

"Of course not. What good would that do? I would only make her uncomfortable." Lenore was silent for a moment.

"By the way," she asked, "if you had found the money, would you have reported it to the police?"

"I don't know," I said. "Would you?"

She smiled and said, "Not if I needed it as badly as her father did."

At that moment the nurse approached. "Mrs. Strafferd," she said, "it's time to move you so that your hip doesn't stiffen."

Lenore smiled at me and said, "Thank you, nurse."